Keys to Your Golden Years

TOOLS FOR A SUCCESSFUL RETIREMENT

Brett King

Elite Financial Associates
TAMPA, FLORIDA

Copyright © 2016 by Brett King.

All rights reserved. No part of this publication may be reproduced, distributed or transmitted in any form or by any means, including photocopying, recording, or other electronic or mechanical methods, without the prior written permission of the publisher, except in the case of brief quotations embodied in critical reviews and certain other noncommercial uses permitted by copyright law. For permission requests, write to the publisher at the address below.

Brett King/Elite Financial Associates
550 N. Reo Street 300
Tampa, FL 33609
www.elitefinancialassociates.com

Book layout ©2013 BookDesignTemplates.com

Ordering information:
Available on Amazon.com. For details, contact the publisher at the address above.

Keys to Your Golden Years/ Brett King. —1st ed.
ISBN 978-1539372097

Contents

Chapter One: The Early Years: Becoming the Best at What I Do ... 5

Chapter Two: Finding the "Perfect" Financial Advisor 11

Chapter Three: Investment Options and Diversification 23

Chapter Four: Roadblocks to a Successful Retirement 33

Chapter Five: Using the Tax Code to Your Advantage 47

    Individual Retirement Account 49

    401(k) Plan 50

    Other Tax-Advantaged Ways to Invest: 55

    For the Self-Employed 57

Chapter Six: Protecting What You Have: Risk vs. Reward 59

    Inflation 64

    Retirement Budget 65

    Guaranteed Income 66

Chapter Seven: Understanding Annuities 101 71

Chapter Eight: Social Security 83

Chapter Nine: Rollovers - It's Your Money, Take It With You .. 91

    Increase Your Options 93

    Expenses and Fees 95

Required Minimum Distributions 96

Flexibility..97

Chapter Ten: Creating an Income Plan 99

You Must Know What You Can Safely Withdraw................102

People Who Have Not Saved Enough 104

Chapter Eleven: The Importance of Wills, Trusts and Estate Planning..109

What Is Estate Planning? 111

Chapter Twelve: In Conclusion 115

ACKNOWLEDGEMENTS

It has been suggested many times by many different people that I share my years of experience in the financial services industry by writing a book, and finally — after additional prodding by my family — the result is what you are about to read in the upcoming chapters.

I would like to take the time to acknowledge some of the people who helped make this long overdue project a reality. Let me start off by recognizing Rodney Brooks, a long-time financial writer for USA Today who helped me put my thoughts into words on many occasions, as well as researching much of the statistical facts you will see in this book.

A special thanks to my wife of 35 years, Judy, for putting up with me on many nights and weekends while writing this, as I'm sure she would've rather had us spend that time doing things together.

I'd also like to thank my children, David and MaryBeth, for inspiring me to continue making progress to finish this manuscript. David would often proofread each chapter to make sure they were correct.

Many thanks also go out to Bill Kentling of 65669 Writer's Guild, along with the Creative SuperGroup team at Advisors Creative in Topeka, Kansas, for making this book possible. Without their combined talents, along with much continued encouragement, this book wouldn't have ever materialized.

Finally, I'd like to thank all of my clients for allowing me the privilege of servicing their financial and investment needs for over three decades. Without the complete trust and confidence they have placed in me, none of this would have been possible.

Enjoy the book. …

CHAPTER ONE

The Early Years: Becoming the Best at What I Do

After working 35 years in financial services, I sometimes reflect on all the people I've been fortunate enough to have met and helped in securing the retirement they have dreamed about, deserved and worked so hard to achieve. My sincere desire in writing this book is that my experience with my friends and my clients will empower you with the knowledge to forge your own path to the retirement of your dreams.

One of the things that still drives me today is my father's death at age 50, leaving my mother — who had been a homemaker — a young widow with no savings and no income beyond the small widow's pension she would receive from the steel mill where he had worked for 15 years.

For me, it all started in the City of Good Neighbors: Buffalo, New York — or, as we liked to refer to it, the Miami of the North. (Hey, when you have to shovel 200 inches of snow some winters, you have to develop a sense of humor.)

We were pretty poor. I was born when my mother was in her mid-30s. I had two sisters and a brother, but they were all much older than me. We lived in the Lower West Side of Buffalo. It was a rough neighborhood back then, but today I'm not sure I would even drive through it.

My father, Larry King, had little education. He drove a taxi cab for a while, but his first big job was at Bethlehem Steel. They had a really big operation in Lackawanna, New York. At its peak in the 1970s, Bethlehem had 35,000 employees. So, by the time I was 8 or 9, we were able to move to a little better part of town.

Things were going well. He was getting promotions, eventually becoming a supervisor in the blast furnace department. But my father was not well. He had myasthenia gravis, a neuromuscular disease. After about 10 years, it caught up with him. For the next three or four years he would be on and off of work. Finally, at 50, he succumbed. The official cause of death was a massive heart attack.

I'm telling this story so you can understand where I got this drive and determination to make sure people are better prepared to retire. We weren't ready, and I watched my mother suffer the consequences.

My mother was too young for Social Security, and she had to fight for the little bit of pension that she got, which was around $150 to $200 a month. My father was just shy of 15 years at the mill, so they had to make an exception for her to even qualify for that.

They had no savings, but he left her with a small group life insurance policy. My brother and sisters were in the early stages of their careers, so they were not able to provide a lot of assistance. I had just recently moved back home, but I was young — having just turned 19. So I was not able to provide much financial help.

We knew there was no way my mother could afford to stay in her current home, so the family decided it made more sense for her to buy a two-family place in the city where prices were much more affordable. She lived in the lower apartment, and rented out the upper unit to help pay the mortgage.

Having to deal with not only the grief of losing a man she was married to for 30 years and simultaneously having to give up her home is something no one should ever have to deal with.

My father never planned. We all know we are mortal, but he didn't give it enough thought. People back then did not plan very much.

Most families had sole breadwinners. Retirement plans were defined-benefit plans. And you had Social Security. That's what people lived on. There wasn't a lot of planning, but as time went on, things started changing.

The only real financial planning my father ever ascribed to was dreaming of the day he would retire, perhaps at 65, though ironically, the factory where he had worked was closed before he would have turned 62. He owned no personal life insurance and only minimal group insurance through Bethlehem Steel. He had no personal savings, nor any retirement savings other than what his employer contributed to. That, as my mother found out the hard way, was not nearly enough to survive on.

After being out of the work force for nearly 30 years while raising her family, my mother was forced to take whatever odd jobs she could to make ends meet. She never learned to drive. She took a job at the neighborhood dry cleaners, which was two or three blocks away from her new home.

This had a profound impact on me as a young man, and I believe my decision to enter the financial services field was a direct result of my desire to help families properly plan their financial road map in the hopes that they would never have to face the kinds of decisions my mother was forced to make, all while still grieving over losing the only man she ever loved.

It affected me strongly. I didn't want other people to have to go through something like that. I wanted to help them plan better. I wanted people to focus on thinking about what could happen. Most people in that situation don't have time to grieve because they have to make potentially life-changing decisions.

While my father's death pushed me into the industry, it was my first experience after hanging my own shingle that had a profound impact on the kind of financial planner I am today.

Shortly after entering the industry, I was faced with helping someone who had been taken advantage by someone he thought was helping him. That was my first experience with how some unethical planners could damage a family and ruin the reputation of an entire profession.

My first real job was with a real estate rental relocation office, but it was in Syracuse, New York, a city that can make Buffalo winters seem rather mild by comparison. I had to look for a career, and I was now married. Then, in 1982, I was offered my first job in financial services, with McCormick and Associates. I quickly accepted. They were well known for having one of the best training programs in the entire region.

Buffalo was three hours down the New York State Thruway from Syracuse. My wife, Judy, was homesick, and both of our families were there. So, every weekend we were making that three-hour drive, even in the winter. One time they shut down the Thruway. We were stuck for two hours. Another time it took us eight hours. We were driving 15 miles an hour with our newborn son strapped into the car seat.

Within 18 months, I was offered a chance to enter McCormick's management training program, which I gave much consideration to. But the independent side of me yearned to run my own firm. Both our families were in Buffalo, so we returned there in 1983, and I started my own agency in July of that year.

One of the first potential clients I met after I returned to Buffalo was a plastic surgeon who had just completed his residency and opened a private practice. During our conversation, he mentioned that a few years earlier a local financial advisor had sold him and many other medical residents a financed life insurance policy that allowed him to secure a large amount of insurance coverage while paying very small premiums.

On the surface, this sounded like a great idea since he had a wife and two small children to look out for in the event of his demise. However, the advisor failed to document and fully explain to this young doctor that the reason he was paying such a minimal amount out of pocket for the insurance was the fact he was borrowing large amounts of money at high interest rates to make up the policy premium difference.

To make matters worse, he would soon be required to repay what now amounted to a sizeable loan balance at the very time he could least afford it. Virtually all of his money had been spent opening up his new medical practice.

Being young and new to this business, I was appalled at what seemed to be a deliberate attempt on that advisor's part to put his own needs (and a large commission) before those of his client's. He failed to completely explain to this doctor exactly what he was getting into, making it impossible for him to make a proper decision.

After showing me a letter he had just received from his insurance company demanding he repay this massive loan, I suggested we work together and draft a letter to his insurance company explaining, in detail, the lack of disclosure provided by his advisor, who was also acting as their representative. That, in our eyes amounted to fraud.

Several weeks after the letter was submitted, I received a call from this young doctor, who was ecstatic, saying the response he received from the insurance company was better than we had expected. Not only did they forgive his loan entirely, but he also received a refund check for all the premiums he had paid out of his own pocket, as well.

The letter apologized for any trauma this experience may have caused him and his family, and indicated they would further investigate their representative's sales practices to make certain this didn't happen to anyone else. A few years later, I heard that advisor had been barred from our industry for life, as it should be.

This business is about helping people by coming up with the best solutions available to solve their personal financial needs, which is what I've strived to do since the very beginning of my career.

And what about that young doctor? He continues to be a loyal client and friend since the day he received that letter lifting the onerous burden of that huge loan from his shoulders and mind. He has through the years often shared with his friends and colleagues positive comments about the work I've done for him, and, as of this writing, plans to retire within the next year. I get great pleasure from knowing I helped him reach his retirement goal.

Examples like this and many others throughout the years have taught me a very valuable lesson: Always putting clients' needs and goals ahead of your own will reward you tenfold over time.

Much has changed through the years. For the past 10 years I have lived and worked in Tampa, Florida, with my lovely wife of 35 years, Judy. We have two grown children, David and MaryBeth.

What remains the same, however, is my burning desire to educate and serve my clients through my experience and dedication.

CHAPTER TWO

Finding the "Perfect" Financial Advisor

Choosing the right doctor, dentist or even someone to do your taxes can be both difficult and time consuming. The same may hold true for choosing the right financial advisor. But when you expect to deal with any professional for a long period of time, it's imperative that you take the necessary time to make the right choice for you and your family.

I've found through the years that most people have certain criteria when choosing a financial advisor, and it usually comes down to these basic questions:

1.) Do I like you?
2.) Do I trust you?
3.) Are you an experienced advisor?
4.) What sets you apart from other financial advisors?
5.) Do you have my best interest in mind?
6.) Are you an independent advisor who can offer me unbiased solutions?

When I began my career in 1982, one of the decisions I made was to make myself available to my clients not only during normal business hours, but also evenings and weekends. I still do that today.

Since many people are working longer hours than ever, I feel it's very important to be available — when my clients are available — to answer questions or review investments, especially when markets are volatile, like we've certainly seen in the past few years.

I've come across many stockbrokers over the years who get to their office at 9:30 a.m., when the stock market opens, and leave at 4 p.m., when it closes. They won't take client calls after they've departed, which I find appalling.

With all the choices investors have today as to who manages their money, including robo-advisors, it's imperative for financial professionals like myself to expand their services and availability, not decrease them. Doing the right things for clients by putting their needs first has allowed me the privilege of working with many of my clients' family members, friends, neighbors and colleagues. That has greatly reduced the need for me to spend valuable time and resources advertising for new clients.

This allows me the opportunity to spend even more time on important areas such as client reviews, continuing education, product development and knowledge, as well as researching many of the thousands of investment options available in today's complex financial universe.

When deciding which financial advisor you're going to work with, it's important that you interview that candidate and ask all the questions you need to in order to make an informed decision. What I would suggest you don't do is base your decision entirely from attending some unknown advisor's workshop or dinner seminar, just because you received an invitation, and assume that person is an expert in the financial planning or retirement field.

In the Tampa, Florida, area, where I currently work and reside with my wife, I get five to 10 "free seminar" invitations a week, many of which are from so-called retirement planning specialists who are relatively new in this business. That is, perhaps, what makes it necessary for them to advertise in the hopes of attracting new clients.

They may look and seem sincere in an effort to convince you that their only purpose is to educate their audience, but keep in mind that the average cost for a dinner seminar with 50 attendees at a reasonably nice restaurant is over $5,000. I'll leave it to you, the reader, to draw your own conclusions as to why so many of these "free" dinner seminars are being offered everywhere you look these days.

Perhaps common sense would dictate that the real reason many of these financial seminars are being held in record numbers in cities across the U.S. might be for the benefit of the financial advisor to acquire new client assets, which most likely will lead to increased fees and commissions for him or her.

To be absolutely clear, I am in no way implying that all financial seminars are bad or held for nefarious reasons. Nor am I suggesting that a majority of financial advisors who put on these seminars are unscrupulous. In fact, the majority of them are fine professionals looking to expand their business practices.

I'm merely suggesting that you not place too much emphasis on how good a public speaker that advisor may be, and not limit yourself in gathering additional information on someone who will be playing such an important role in your financial future's success or failure.

To give you a personal perspective on this very topic, I recently received a call from a longtime client who attended one of these seminars with her husband. They were under the impression that it was a tax-reduction seminar, yet within five minutes after it began, it was clear that the focus was on selling annuities to attendees. The advisor who hosted the event subsequently recommended to my client that she surrender her existing annuity contract and purchase a different one offered by the advisor's firm.

During my conversation with my client, I was able to ascertain that this new advisor made this recommendation to her without even reviewing her current annuity contract thoroughly. Had this new advisor done so, he would have realized my client's existing annuity had built up substantial living benefit income and death benefits through policy riders over the past 13 years she has owned it, and she would have lost those benefits if she had taken his ill-conceived advice and surrendered her annuity!

Clearly this advisor was far more interested in the commissions this proposed exchange would generate for him, rather than considering the client's best interest and the consequences she would have faced had she listened to his poorly conceived recommendation.

Don't get me wrong. Any and all professions have their good and bad apples. But I could cite many more examples of the unscrupulous acts I've witnessed and heard about through the years from financial advisors that have no business giving advice, and clearly shouldn't be licensed to sell investments or insurance.

When new clients come to me for the first time, it's usually because they are unhappy with their current advisor. They don't feel like the advisor is looking out for them. They are not being proactive, and they do not feel like he or she is managing their accounts properly.

What I hear frequently is "he only calls me when he wants to sell me something," or "she doesn't do reviews of my financial plan." They hear or read what an advisor is supposed to do for them and they don't feel they are getting that. A lot of them feel their advisors are ignoring them because their account is not big enough.

I have one client who, every time I go to her house, tells me she doesn't know why I take such good care of her and her husband when their accounts aren't that big, and I always respond "because you're both important to me regardless of the size of your portfolio."

Most of my clients have become my friends as well over the years. I've been to many of their homes for dinner and attended numerous family gatherings, including weddings, birthdays and anniversaries, just to name a few. It's not just a business relationship. I have never set minimum asset requirements in order to be willing to help someone plan their financial future, and I give all my clients the same level of service regardless of their assets. In turn, they have rewarded me by referring family members, friends, neighbors and business colleagues, which has allowed my business to grow substantially over the years.

It's a good idea to ask your potential new advisor about referrals. Every advisor will have clients who won't mind sharing their experiences with you.

In fact, my business at this point of my career is mostly referrals. It's almost 100 percent word of mouth. It allows me to focus more time on existing clients. I still have a large client base in my hometown of Buffalo, New York, and when I relocated to Florida more than a decade ago, my goal was to retain those clients. Oftentimes when a financial advisor relocates to another state, there's a good chance they will lose many of their existing clients within five to 10 years, since many of those clients may prefer dealing with a local advisor, but I've been able to keep the majority of mine due to the relationships we've forged. I still to this day go back to Buffalo four to six times a year to meet with these clients, usually from 6 or 7 a.m. in the morning until late in the evening. I firmly believe that this ongoing dedication to the welfare of my clients is the reason my retention level has remained so high throughout the years.

My largest account, in terms of asset size, is a doctor who lives in Houston, Texas, whom I helped with a complex financial situation many years ago, receiving no financial compensation. She was so surprised that I was willing and able to help her accomplish what she desired without any fee, she subsequently asked me to manage all of her investments and set up a pension plan for her employees as well.

This doctor and her husband have been clients and friends for close to 30 years. Their son and his wife, both physicians, are now also my clients.

What does that tell you? If you do the right thing and help people, and put their needs first, it comes back to you tenfold. You can't go into a meeting, referral or a relationship asking, "What will I get out of this?" You want a long-term client relationship, so if you do what's right for them by putting their needs first, you will have a loyal client for life. This is how I've run my practice for more than three decades, leading to my high client retention level. Industry statistics show that the average client stays with their broker for only five years, or they have more than one broker handling their investment portfolio.

It comes back to the questions I raised earlier in this chapter, especially No. 4: What sets you apart? Some of the stories I am sharing with you is what sets me apart from other brokers and financial advisors. When I first got into this business, I made a conscious effort to be available whenever my clients need me. As stated earlier in this chapter, many brokers are there when the stock exchange is open, and after the closing bell they don't want to be bothered. I've heard many tell their assistants as they prepare to leave their office, "If any clients call, tell them I'll get back to them tomorrow."

People are busier than ever these days. We have far more two-worker households than any previous generation. Clients call me at home many times after 8 or 9 p.m. I always take their calls and answer their questions because I understand the long hours they're working as well, trying to support their families and prepare for retirement. That's what I believe sets me apart — not only what I'm doing, but my accessibility. I want long-lasting relationships with my clients. People are looking for somebody they can trust and identify with, somebody who will listen to them. I know a lot of advisors who do 80 percent of the talking when they meet new clients. I learned that in order to be a good advisor you have to be a great listener. You have to let them share what they are looking for, what they expect from their advisor, what they expect from the relationship, what their dreams and goals are for their retirement years. I have found through experience, if you do that, they will most certainly like you and will start trusting you. Trust is earned over time.

It doesn't happen in the first meeting. That meeting should be at least an hour, depending on how complex one's situation is. Some people have done a good job of investing. You may be talking about the best Social Security options, or how they can maximize savings now.

Sometimes that first meeting can last for two hours or even longer. I recall the longest meeting I ever had was in Buffalo. I was meeting with an OB/GYN. He was called away to deliver four babies, and our initial meeting ended up lasting 5 ½ hours!

I have always spent as much time as necessary, since an initial meeting is also a fact-finding mission, a time to gather a financial history of information to better serve clients. Most people are familiar with the old adage that, in order for a physician to properly treat their patient's medical conditions, they need as much information as possible, including previous medical records, test results and, of course, those annoying multiple-page new patient information packets that seem to take forever to fill out. The very same thing holds true when it comes to your financial health check-up.

A seasoned financial advisor should be consulted to review your entire profile, including but not limited to:
- Your current income and expenses
- Assets including existing investments
- Individual and employer-sponsored retirement plans
- Your investment objectives and risk tolerance
- Current insurance policies, including life, health, disability and long-term-care coverages
- Social Security statements provided by the Social Security Administration, detailing your earnings history and projecting your future benefit amounts, depending on the year you begin collecting benefits.

Once you've shared all of this pertinent information with your financial advisor, he or she can begin to put together an appropriate and complete financial plan personalized just for you.

Remember, just like in the physician example above, if you withhold important information and details from your financial advisor, it will be nearly impossible for him or her to provide you with an accurate blueprint for financial success. You only get out what you put into the process.

Throughout my career spanning nearly 35 years, there have been instances when I'm first meeting potential new clients where they may be reluctant to share all of their financial information so early in the process, perhaps due to personal privacy reasons or other family issues. But I explain to them why it's necessary and to their benefit for me to be able to see their entire financial picture in order for my expertise to be worthwhile in producing an accurate plan.

This process reminds me of another profound old adage: "garbage in, garbage out," which simply means that if complete and accurate information is not input, then the output is almost certainly going to be inaccurate and useless.

Your new advisor will review all of these items and help you establish your investment objective, risk tolerance, time horizon and retirement income plan among other things.

Any retirement income plan should provide guaranteed income for life for you and your spouse if married, regardless of how long you or your spouse may live, especially considering how much longer people are living nowadays than in previous generations. Studies show that the biggest fear that retirees face is running out of money and being forced to live on Social Security alone, which we all know was never established to be the only source of retirement income for Americans. In fact, it accounts for only a third of the average person's overall retirement income.

Other factors that need to be included in any retirement income plan are health care costs, which are spiraling out of control and can be one of the largest expenses retirees face.

Will you still be covered by your employer's plan after you retire and, if so, for how long? Will you need to rely on Medicare coverage and a Medicare Supplement policy to fill in the gaps Medicare benefits don't cover? That can amount to another $10,000-plus per year in out-of-pocket expenses!

Inflation must also be taken into consideration when determining income needs at retirement. If your income plan doesn't provide cost-of-living adjustments (COLAs) to keep up with annual inflation, your buying power and standard of living will be greatly diminished. Most government data suggest that the annual inflation rate lies somewhere between 2-3 percent annually, but the unfortunate reality for retirees is that most of the expenses they pay for out of pocket have been rising at a much higher rate than those government figures show. Among those expenses: health care costs, utilities, property taxes, food and clothing.

It is also highly recommended that potential long-term-care costs be accounted for in any retirement plan, either through the purchase of a long-term-care insurance policy or the earmarking of funds to cover these potential costs. Statistically speaking, a husband and wife both age 65 have a 50 percent chance that one of them will need long-term care during their retirement years. Whether it be a skilled nursing facility, assisted living or home care needs, the costs are usually staggering and can destroy the best of financial plans if provisions have not been made ahead of time.

Even though this can seem overwhelming, working with the correct financial advisor can certainly make the entire process easier and less painful. The good news is, once your plan is established, monitoring it going forward becomes much easier. Your advisor should be meeting with you at least annually and taking care of keeping your plan current and updated.

One of the important questions to ask any potential financial advisor is how they are paid. Some are fee-based, others are commission-based. Some may charge for setting up a financial plan for you that must be implemented through another source. Ask what types of licenses they have. Their licenses will dictate what types of investments they can offer to you. Ideally, you should work with an independent advisor who is licensed in as many financial services possible and unencumbered with limitations on the kinds of investment and/or insurance products and advice offered.

There will be areas such as legal and tax services where your financial advisor will need to reach out to other professionals in those fields for your benefit. This team-based approach, in my opinion, is the best way to benefit clients, since no one person can possibly be an expert in every field. It's far better to have top experts in their fields on your team than one person having just some knowledge in many fields.

For this very reason, a few years back I teamed up with a firm from San Diego, California, called Elite Resource Team. They work with CPAs and financial advisors all over the country to provide more holistic planning through a nationwide team of experts in areas such as tax mitigation, business valuations and financing, insurance captive agent programs for businesses, premium financing and many other complex specialized planning areas for the benefit of our clients.

In addition, I have an affiliation with Advisors Excel, located in Topeka, Kansas, the nation's largest insurance and annuity financial marketing organization with more than 75 of the best carriers in the industry, thus providing my clients with nearly unlimited choices.

Advisors Excel is four times larger — from a premium production standpoint — than the next-closest competitor, which has allowed them to design and market some of the very best fixed index annuities and fixed index universal life policies available, some of which are proprietary and only available through their chosen appointed representatives like myself, a big advantage for my clients to have!

To summarize, finding the right financial advisor to work with for the rest of your life can be almost as important as any of the actual investments you own in your retirement portfolio.

CHAPTER THREE

Investment Options and Diversification

In the previous chapter, we discussed the importance of choosing the right financial advisor. One of the most important reasons is that advisor must be able to explain to you the variety of investment options in today's complex financial markets, and how some of these options may play an important role in the success of your retirement planning.

There are tens of thousands of available stocks, bonds, mutual funds, exchange-traded funds (ETFs) and the like, for investors to choose from. That's why it's more important than ever to receive knowledgeable guidance from a professional who will match your investment objectives and risk tolerance with the appropriate and well-diversified investment options.

You may ask yourself "what is diversification and why is it important to me?" It may, in fact, be the most important aspect of your investment portfolio. Diversification simply means the process of allocating your investments in a variety of assets. The purpose is to reduce exposure and/or volatility.

In layman's terms, it is the principle of not putting all your eggs in one basket. I can't think of a better example of how devastating this can be than the Enron bankruptcy of 2001. Many employees of this energy company behemoth were being told by management how great the company was doing. As a result, many invested most or all of their 401(k) retirement money in company stock rather than other options offered by the plan.

The company stock reached a high of $90.75 in mid-2000, only to crash to $1 in November 2001. On Dec. 2, 2001, Enron filed what was, at that time, the largest corporate bankruptcy in U.S. history. (It was surpassed by WorldCom the following year.)

What resulted from this debacle? For Enron employees who chose to invest most or all of their 401(k) retirement money in their company's stock, it was a total loss. There were reports at that time of employees getting ready to retire from Enron thinking they had, at a minimum, some $1 million in their 401(k) plans, only to find they were completely wiped out. If it wasn't bad enough news that many couldn't retire as previously planned, it was also apparent that these almost-retirees would now have to find new jobs, adding insult to injury.

Had these Enron employees diversified their 401(k) retirement plans by spreading the risk over multiple investment options, the outcome for most would have been completely different.

Most people are aware that investing in non-guaranteed securities carries the risk of partial or total loss, but when you diversify by spreading your investments over different asset categories, you are reducing your risk of a total loss.

Let's assume those Enron employees who chose to invest 100 percent of their 401(k) in company stock had instead diversified by investing only 10 percent in Enron stock. If they spread out the balance to other investment options offered by their plan, their losses would have been 10 percent, not 100 percent, when Enron collapsed into bankruptcy.

Sure, a 10 percent portfolio loss right at or near the time of retirement might put a dent in one's plans, but certainly is not as catastrophic as losing your entire 401(k) retirement account overnight. That's the power of having a properly diversified investment portfolio, and the main reason why it's so important if you want to increase your odds of living your retirement dream.

The right financial advisor will be able to help you navigate through the myriad of options and suggest an appropriate and well-diversified investment portfolio tailored to your individual needs, while also assisting you to stay on course in the future.

Rather than make this an exercise in trying to explain every different investment offered on planet Earth, I will instead cover some of the more common types of investments that may play an important role in your financial and/or retirement plan. Your financial advisor can help determine further which types of options may be suitable for you and your family.

Stocks

A stock is a security that signifies ownership in a corporation and represents a claim on part of that corporation's assets and earnings. There are two main types of stock: Common and preferred. Common stock usually entitles the owner to vote at shareholders' meetings and receive dividends. Preferred stock generally does not have voting rights, but has a higher claim on assets and earnings than the common shares. For example, owners of preferred stock receive dividends before common shareholders and have priority in the event that a company goes bankrupt and is liquidated.

Bonds

A bond is a debt investment in which an investor loans money to an entity (typically corporate or governmental), which borrows those funds for a set period of time, at a variable or fixed interest rate. Bonds are used by companies, municipalities, states and sovereign governments to raise money and finance a variety of projects and activities. Owners of bonds are debtholders, or creditors, of the issuer. Bonds are commonly referred to as fixed-income securities.

Mutual Funds

A mutual fund is an investment vehicle that is made up of a pool of funds collected from many investors for the purpose of investing in securities such as stocks, bonds, money market instruments and similar assets. Mutual funds are operated by money managers who invest the fund's capital and attempt to produce capital gains and income for the fund's investors. A mutual fund's portfolio is structured and maintained to match the investment objectives stated in the prospectus. One of the main advantages of mutual funds is that they give small investors access to professionally managed, diversified portfolios of equities, bonds and other securities, which would be difficult (if not impossible) to create with a small amount of capital.

Exchange-Traded Funds (ETFs)

An ETF, or exchange-traded fund, is a marketable security that tracks an index, a commodity, bonds or a basket of assets like an index fund. Unlike mutual funds, an ETF trades like a common stock on a stock exchange. ETFs experience price changes throughout the day as they are bought and sold. ETFs typically have higher daily liquidity and lower fees than mutual fund shares, making them an attractive alternative for individual investors.

Unit Investment Trusts (UITs)

An investment company that offers a fixed, unmanaged portfolio, generally of stocks and bonds, as redeemable "units" to investors for a specific period of time. It is designed to provide capital appreciation and/or dividend income. Each unit typically costs $1,000 and is sold to investors by brokers.

Alternative Investments

An investment that is not one of the three traditional asset types (stocks, bonds and cash). Most alternative investment assets are held by institutional investors or accredited, high-net-worth individuals because of their complex nature, limited regulations and relative lack of liquidity. Alternative investments include hedge funds, managed futures, real estate, commodities and derivatives contracts. Many alternative investments also have high minimum investments and fee structures compared to mutual funds and ETFs.

Structured Products

A structured product, also known as a market-linked investment, is a pre-packaged investment strategy based on derivatives, such as a single security, a basket of securities, options, indices, commodities, debt issuance and/or foreign currencies, and to a lesser extent, swaps. There is no single, uniform definition of a structured product. A feature of some structured products is a "principal guarantee" function, which offers protection of principal if held to maturity. The risks associated with many structured products are similar to risks involved with options. Principal-protected products are not always insured by the FDIC. They may only be insured by the issuer, and thus could potentially lose the principal if there is a liquidity crisis or bankruptcy.

Separately Managed Accounts

An SMA is a portfolio of assets under the management of a professional investment firm. In the United States, the vast majority of such firms are called Registered Investment Advisors. One or more portfolio managers are responsible for day-to-day investment decisions, supported by a team of analysts, operations and administrative staff.

Private Placements

Private placement (or non-public offering) is a funding round of securities that are sold not through a public offering, but rather through a private offering, mostly to a small number of chosen investors. Although these placements are subject to the Securities Act of 1933, the securities offered do not have to be registered with the Securities and Exchange Commission. Investors should have a sufficient financial knowledge and experience to be capable of evaluating the risks and merits of investing in a company.

Fixed Annuities

A fixed annuity is an insurance contract that allows the holder a fixed return for the life of the annuity. Like any annuity, a person buys into a policy, either with a lump sum or premiums over a period of time. When that person reaches a certain age, or retirement (whichever is greater) he or she begins to receive payments. Typically, the insurance company issuing a fixed annuity invests the premiums in low-risk investment vehicles such as bonds. This results in a smaller likelihood that the insurance company will be unable to make the payments, but also exposes the holder to inflation risk.

Variable Annuities

A variable annuity is an insurance company product designed to allow you to accumulate retirement savings. It provides a small guaranteed return for the life of the annuity, along with another return that depends on the performance of a portfolio. Like any annuity, an individual buys into a policy, either with a lump sum or premiums over a period of time. When he or she reaches a certain age, or retirement (whichever is greater), he or she begins to receive payments. Generally speaking, the insurance company issuing the variable annuity invests the premiums in investment vehicles such as stocks or mutual funds. This exposes the holder to risk that he or she will be stuck with a smaller return, but also carries the possibility of a much larger return.

Fixed Index Annuities

A fixed index annuity is a type of annuity that grows at the greater of

a.   An annual, guaranteed minimum rate of return, or

b.   The return from a specified stock market index such as the S&P 500, reduced by certain expenses and formulas.

At the time the contract is opened, a term is chosen (the number of years until the principal is guaranteed and the surrender period ends). In a robust stock market, you will not achieve the actual performance of the index due to the formulas, spread, participation rates and caps applied to fixed index annuities, as well as the absence of dividends. However, in a down market you won't lose principal, provided the underlying insurance company stays solvent, and to date no insurance company has ever failed to pay out on a fixed annuity. Many investors find that fixed index annuity returns closely approximate CDs, traditional fixed annuities or high-grade bonds, but with the potential for a small hedge against inflation in an up market.

As you can see from these examples, different investments come with varying degrees of risk and potential for gains or losses. It is generally suggested that as people age and get nearer to retirement, the amount of overall risk in their investment portfolio should decrease.

This makes perfect sense when you consider that, if a person is within a few years of retirement and suffers a huge market loss in their portfolio due to too much risk, they most likely will not have enough time to recover those losses prior to retirement.

My philosophy with clients nearing their retirement years has always been to protect whatever assets they currently have, especially those assets that will be needed to provide them the maximum amount possible of guaranteed income for life, while still providing the potential for future growth as well as cost-of-living income adjustments.

People often ask me how much money, in lump-sum terms, they'll need to retire comfortably. I think the more important question to ask is how much income they will need for the rest of their lives to retire comfortably.

If you're merely trying to calculate a lump-sum figure to retire with, you may be missing the bigger picture. More important is whether or not that lump-sum amount will be sufficient to provide enough income every month for the rest of your life, not only to pay regular expenses but also cover those extras that most of us desire for our Golden Years.

Imagine for a moment that the day you decide to retire, you cash in all your investments and place those funds under your bed. The idea is you'll take from that pile whenever money is needed to pay bills, take a vacation or buy groceries. There wouldn't possibly be a way to determine the likelihood of you outliving your funds under that scenario, which is clearly why I haven't seen anyone actually try it.

You may be scared to death of the stock market and its volatile swings. Or maybe you're avoiding bonds for fear that interest rates might be going up. Or, perhaps, you have heard or read something negative about a certain type of annuity.

The simple truth is, most people have nowhere near enough money saved for retirement to be able to live off the interest paid by bank accounts or CDs in this historically low interest rate environment. As a result, it has become more important than ever for financial advisors to become more knowledgeable about alternative strategies for the benefit of their clients. We must work closer than ever with clients to set up diversified portfolios that provide monthly distributions for life, while still meeting their investment objectives and risk tolerances.

The ideal retirement plan, in my view, is one that clearly defines what income a retiree will receive every month and where that income will come from. It should also indicate where the necessary cost-of-living increases will come from to keep pace with inflation, so that buying power isn't eroded.

CHAPTER FOUR

Roadblocks to a Successful Retirement

In previous generations, retirement plans were mainly defined benefit plans, or pensions, that were funded solely by employers. You knew if you worked a certain number of years and you were a certain age, when you retired you had a fixed benefit amount.

All of that has changed over the past several decades. Many company plans were underfunded, and they said they could no longer afford to provide this benefit to their employees. That resulted in the onset of 401(k)s, or defined-contribution plans, that are primarily funded by you, the employee. Even though some companies match up to a certain percentage of your contributions, you, the employee, are still funding the majority of it.

The burden has now shifted from the employer to you, the employee. As I write this book in August of 2016, about 18 percent of full-time workers have pensions, down from 35 percent in the early 1990s, according to the Bureau of Labor Statistics.

Managing your retirement portfolio is certainly not easy and there are so many things that can go wrong. That's one reason it is so important to get a good financial advisor to help you.

So, in this chapter, we will talk about the things that can keep you from having a safe and successful retirement, or, at the very least, things that can make your retirement more difficult than it has to be.

What should be apparent is, it's not that hard to do the things that are necessary, but ignoring the hazards on this list can be disastrous for your retirement.

Not Saving Enough

Let's start with what is one of the most common retirement killers, but is also one of the easiest to fix. And that's the fact that most American workers don't save enough.

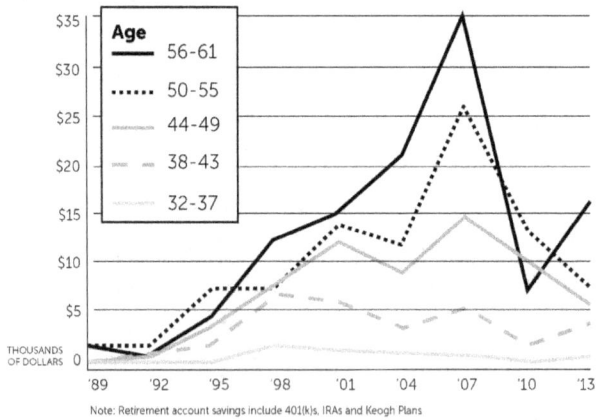

RETIREMENT SAVINGS ACCOUNTS
Most families, even those approaching retirement, have little or no retirement savings. Nearly half of families have no retirement savings, making the median (50th percentile) values low for all age groups. Median by age group:

Note: Retirement account savings include 401(k)s, IRAs and Keogh Plans

The U.S. household savings rate was 4 percent in 2015, according to the Organization for Economic Cooperation and Development. That compares to an average of 8 percent in the European Union, 9.3 percent in Australia and 9.7 percent in Germany.

It's clear that the U.S. savings rate is among the lowest of all industrialized nations. Tie that to the fact that we are living longer due to medical breakthroughs and you have a recipe for retirement disaster.

That all leads to an increased chance that retirees will run out of money and be forced to live on Social Security alone, which in most cases would not be sufficient to maintain your current lifestyle. Remember, the purpose of Social Security is to supplement a retirees' income, not be the sole source of it.

So, it now comes down to hard choices. You either retire when you want, but with far less money than you probably need, or continue working in an attempt to reach your retirement income goal.

I had a client who came to me about 12 years ago, right after the stock market crash of 2000 to 2002. She was 70 years old and her husband had recently passed away. He had left her very little money, and the little she had lost a lot of its value during the market crash because their portfolio was overexposed to the stock market. This left us in a difficult situation. Do we keep her invested aggressively due to her current portfolio not being sufficient to provide enough retirement income, or protect her remaining assets to prevent further potential losses?

We decided the prudent approach was to reallocate her portfolio to make it more conservative, even though there wasn't enough money left over to invest after the market crash for her to retire comfortably without working part time. Obviously, I could have said we have to be super aggressive and try to make the money back, but that would have been foolish. In fact, it could easily have made matters worse.

Today she still works part-time, collects Social Security and draws income from the conservative investment portfolio that we reallocated.

The moral of this story: You need to start saving as early as possible, well before your planned retirement date. It is also imperative for both spouses to be aware of their financial circumstances, and work together with a financial advisor to plan ahead for their financial future!

Not Having Your Retirement Portfolio Monitored Properly

In many cases when investments are originally set up, there is no initial monitoring, checking of performance, manager changes, or fees being imposed on those investments. Lots of times this is how I find they don't match a person's investment objectives, state in life, or current risk-tolerance level.

As you get closer to retirement it usually makes sense to reallocate portfolios toward more conservative investments. For many Americans, 401(k) accounts represent the largest retirement asset they own, yet I have found that when I'm meeting with pre-retirees, oftentimes they are unaware of how these assets are invested or what funds they chose to invest in when they began putting money into their 401(k) plan(s).

I have found that, in many cases, what happens is that employees are provided enrollment forms to sign up for their company-sponsored 401(k) retirement plan and given brochures on the investment options. From this, they are expected to make decisions (on their own) about which funds their payroll deductions should be invested into. There may be meetings pulled together by the 401(k) administrator, but they are not usually tailored to each individual employee's situation. The final decision rests with the employee, who, not surprisingly, is not prepared to make that kind of decision.

Oftentimes this may lead employees to choose the funds they want their 401(k) or 403(b) contributions to be invested in by looking back at historical track records of available fund choices offered by their plan, and selecting ones that have had the highest investment returns in the past. That may not be the optimal way to do it, since those funds may have taken on a lot of risk in order to have achieved that past performance. Keep in mind, funds that may have outperformed the market in the past can still perform poorly in the future. That's one of the reasons that in every mutual fund prospectus you will find the required disclosure stating that "past performance is not a guarantee of future performance"

Your financial advisor should be able to assist you in choosing which funds may be appropriate for your unique situation, investment objective(s) and risk-tolerance level. I've always provided this service to my clients, even when I don't directly handle their 401(k) plan. I find it crucial to review what they have and make sure their current investment allocation properly fits their needs and objectives.

Many employees also have a tendency to leave their 401(k)s behind when they leave a job. They often let them stagnate, don't roll them over to an IRA or their current employer's 401(k) plan, and may have no idea what they are invested in. Some people may have various investments all over the place and have no idea of the potential risks they could be facing when they approach retirement.

Among the many advantages of choosing to work closely with a financial advisor is their ability to utilize the tools available today to assist you in making financial decisions now that will affect your future. One of the advantages my clients have is that we use software that can look at their current investment portfolio and assign a risk number, plainly illustrating how much risk they are currently subjected to, and what areas of their portfolio could be changed to meet their risk tolerance and investment objectives.

Many times investors believe they have an adequate level of diversification based solely on the number of funds they own, but oftentimes different funds overlap with each other. Financial advisors have the capability to run reports examining your current portfolio for investment overlaps, thus preventing you from being over-concentrated in only a few areas of the market without even realizing it.

Now, let's talk about both sides of the risk versus reward equation. Some people, especially when young, may be invested far too conservatively, considering their investment time horizon is generally much longer. We as retirement planners are trying to reach out to everybody, old and young. But, since members of the younger generation have a much longer time horizon until their retirement years, they generally have the ability to be more aggressive in their investing. Conversely, people approaching retirement age should consider being invested more conservatively because they will need to access those retirement funds in the near future. It's never a good idea for retirees needing income to have to sell stocks or mutual funds during a bear market.

That's why asset allocation is an absolute necessity. Retirees can't turn back the clock and start over again, so it becomes imperative for them to protect their assets and income sources. Younger investors with longer time horizons usually have the ability to take on more risk for potentially higher returns. Stocks have shown over long periods of time the ability to provide greater average annual returns when compared to bonds or fixed accounts like CDs, with small company stocks leading the way. Between 2010 and 2013, the S&P 500 index, widely considered to be the best gauge of overall U.S. markets, rose at an annualized rate of 16.74 percent. At 15 percent average return per year, it only takes roughly 30 years to turn $15,000 to $1 million. But, and I can't stress this enough, if you have a short-term investment time horizon and/or need to protect your assets, you most likely should not be taking the same level of risk as younger investors that have time on their side.

There's no better example I can provide you than the financial meltdown of 2008. For those people that decided to retire at that time and leave a lot of their money invested in the stock market due to the six-year ongoing bull market, many of these new retirees saw their investment accounts get decimated. Between January 2008 and April 2009, the S&P 500 lost nearly 50 percent of its value. From Oct. 9, 2007, to March 9, 2009, this same index lost 56.6 percent of its value, the worst drop ever in its history.

Even the popular target date funds, which are designed to become more conservatively invested as you approach your retirement date, took a beating in this bear market. As you can see by the following chart, 2010 target date funds didn't protect investors against market losses, some of which were severe, depending on which fund manager a consumer used. The chart also reflects how different fund managers in the exact same target-date-year category perform vastly different, which clearly indicates some funds were exposed to far greater risk than others.

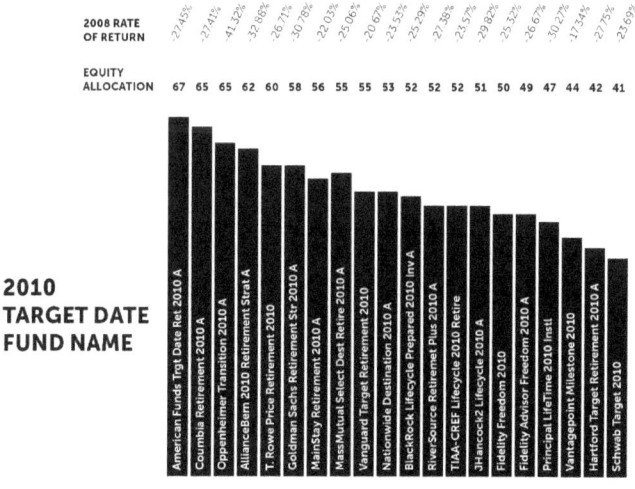

If history teaches us anything, it's a matter of if and not when we see another bear market. With economies around the world including the U.S. being cyclical in nature, there always seems to be times of expansion as well as contraction, which leads to periods of rising bull markets and declining bear markets at some point. I regularly ask pre-retirees what amount or percentage of their investment portfolio they would be comfortable placing at risk, if it meant having the potential for higher returns, and invariably most will answer none. That leads me to recommend, in those instances, more conservative investment options.

Not Understanding Your Investments

We touched on this earlier in the chapter about 401(k) issues and the basic lack of knowledge most employees have to make proper investment decisions within these retirement accounts. Many times in a first meeting with clients, I uncover they have various IRA accounts all over the place with different brokers and financial institutions. They generally have no idea of the totality of these assets and possibly have even forgotten what they're invested in. I find many investors that rarely look at their investment statements in-depth. Often, they are just filed away, not closely looked at, and not reviewed or monitored for accuracy. This tends to happen far more frequently when not working with a financial advisor.

Many investors know they are putting away money for retirement. They assume they'll be OK when the time comes, but they have no way of knowing that for sure without taking on a more active role in their own retirement planning. I'm not suggesting that you need the same knowledge level your financial advisor has obtained through years of study, or that you could ever find the time to acquire such investment knowledge, but I do believe investors have a responsibility to spend the appropriate amount of time to have at least a basic understanding of what they are invested in, and how those investments should benefit them in the long run. Choosing the right financial advisor will make this task easier for you.

Not Having a Tax Strategy

Not understanding how taxes on different investments may affect your overall financial well-being can become a huge roadblock to a successful retirement. As important as it is to have a well-diversified portfolio to mitigate risk, it is equally important to utilize the current investment tax code to your advantage. We'll go into much more detail on this in a later chapter, including tax-deferred versus taxable investing, long-term capital gains taxes as compared to ordinary income tax rates, taxation of traditional IRAs and Roth IRAs, and much more.

Not Understanding Fees

Most investments have fees or commissions associated with them, and it's very important for you to understand how these may affect growing your accounts. Management fees, commissions and sales charges can have an enormous impact on your portfolio.

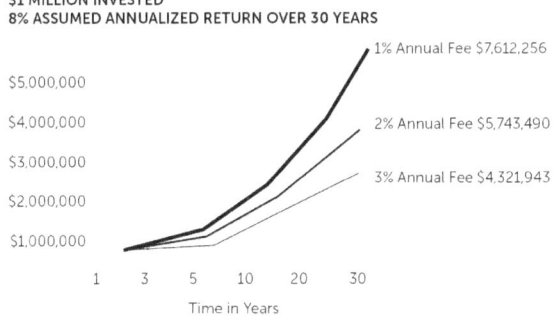

IMPACT OF FEES

$1 MILLION INVESTED
8% ASSUMED ANNUALIZED RETURN OVER 30 YEARS

1% Annual Fee $7,612,256
2% Annual Fee $5,743,490
3% Annual Fee $4,321,943

Time in Years

An article in Forbes magazine looked at the "real cost" of owning a mutual fund and the impact of fees. For instance, Forbes said $1 million invested with an 8 percent assumed annual rate of return over 30 years, with a 1 percent annual management fee, the balance would be $7,612,256. However, with a 2 percent annual fee, the balance drops to $5,743,090. If that annual management fee was 3 percent, the balance would become $4,321,943. That's an astonishing difference, and a great example of how drastically fees can impact growth.

Often considered to be one of the best retirement savings vehicles available, variable annuities often come with some pretty hefty fees. Mortality and expense fees (M&Es) for the issuing insurance company providing a guaranteed death benefit usually range from 1.25 percent to 1.5 percent. There are also fees for optional living benefit riders, also known as income or withdrawal benefit riders that typically cost about 1 percent a year. Enhanced death benefit rider fees, if chosen, typically add another .25 to .50 percent a year. Variable annuity sub-account management fees will run from .50 percent to 1.5 percent on average, depending on the investment sub-accounts selected and the insurance company.

When you add everything up, you can easily get to 3.5–4 percent that you pay in fees each and every year. Those fees are deducted from your actual account performance. I'm not suggesting that variable annuities or other investments with fees are no good, or shouldn't be considered for your portfolio, I'm merely saying you should be aware of any and all fees being charged, what you receive in return for those fees, and what the overall impact may be.

One of the most common investments for the past several decades are called mutual funds. The majority of Americans are familiar or invested in these, either through their employer-sponsored retirement plans or on their own. These are in most cases professionally managed investments that also impose fees. The most common class of mutual funds sold through investment firms are referred to as "A shares," which impose front-load sales charges that can range up to 5.75 percent, depending on the amount of your investment, as well as management fees that again can sometimes exceed 1 percent. Every mutual fund that's doing any kind of trading within that fund incurs trading fees as well. That's like a hidden fee that the consumer doesn't see, or in many cases isn't aware of. These fees can be excessive depending on how much that fund is trading and the portfolio turnover rate of the fund.

Many aggressive equity funds have portfolio turnover rates exceeding 100 percent, which means that during a 12-month period they traded out the equivalent of their entire portfolio. Once again, it's important to be aware of all fees you are paying, whether you pay directly or indirectly.

Lack of Communication

While I believe baby boomer spouses are better at communicating with each other than previous generations did, I still see far too many instances where there is a lack of communication among husbands and wives, particularly when it comes to money, investments or retirement goals and desires. This issue can lead any retirement planning astray, which is why both spouses should sit down with their financial advisor together, so they both completely understand the resources they currently have, as well as their jointly held retirement lifestyle expectations. Still too often when one spouse dies the other one is left in the dark on financial matters, which should never happen in this day and age.

Up until the early 1980s, the majority of workers were men, and when they were ready to retire, their company pension plan normally provided various options on how they could take their pension. These options usually included lump-sum, life-only income on the retiree's life, and some form of joint life option to cover the worker's spouse in the event of their death. Many opted to take the life-only income option since it offered the highest monthly payment.

But the problem was, upon their death the pension payments stopped, with the surviving spouse getting nothing — many times not even being aware this would happen. To avoid this happening any longer, there was a law passed by Congress called the Spousal Consent Law (the Retirement Equity Act of 1984). For IRAs and other retirement plans, in order for the owner of the account to take the life-only option, the spouse has to sign off that they understand all of the consequences involved in doing so, and what benefits they may be forfeiting.

My mother's situation I discussed earlier is a good example of what the lack of communication can do to surviving family members. She had no idea about the family's finances, other than the fact my father left her enough money each week to pay bills. Communication is an absolute key. No one enjoys discussing our own mortality, but we know it to be inevitable, and we must plan for the eventuality that when one spouse pre-deceases the other, the surviving spouse will be taken care of. Don't we owe that much to our significant other?

Long-Term-Care Needs

Your financial advisor may do a fantastic job setting up a retirement and income plan for you, but there is one thing that can derail your plans if it isn't addressed. That's the failure to plan for long-term-care needs. It can absolutely obliterate any financial plan if it's not taken care of, if there is not some provision in your financial plan to provide for the costs of potential future long-term-care needs.

According to the American Association for Long-Term Care Insurance (AALTI), for a couple both 65 years old, the chance that one of them will need long-term care in a staffed facility during their lifetime is 50 percent. Even if you're lucky enough where home health care is an option, it's still extremely expensive.

A financial plan can address this issue in various ways. Purchasing a long-term-care insurance policy can be very expensive, depending on your age. Or there are various life insurance and annuity contracts that may have long-term-care riders attached to them.

Keep in mind: The average stay in a nursing home is 4.7 years…

Inflation

Any successful financial plan and retirement income plan should include provisions for inflation. You don't want to retire with a set amount of income that will not increase. Even if it means you receive that amount monthly or yearly for as long as you live, a static income means your buying power would be severely eroded. We'll talk more about this in a future chapter.

Reduce or Eliminate Debt

You need to reduce your existing debt as much as possible, especially debt that carries high interest rates. That means, if possible, pay off those credit cards and car loans, and if you prefer, and are able to, your mortgage. This will reduce the amount of your retirement income that is earmarked every month to pay bills. Instead, you will have more flexibility to spend that extra income on things you enjoy like travel, hobbies, perhaps a vacation home or even building up your cash reserves. The earlier you begin to manage your debt so that it can be paid off before you retire, the better chance you'll have for a more successful, enjoyable, rewarding and well-deserved retirement.

CHAPTER FIVE

Using the Tax Code to Your Advantage

As mentioned in the previous chapter, with savings rates being so low in the U.S. compared to other industrialized nations, we have to look at other ways to potentially increase future retirement income. Not only should pre-retirees be increasing their savings in the important years before retirement, but they also need to better utilize the current tax code to their advantage, which oftentimes they don't.

You should be able to get that kind of help through your financial advisor. Good financial advisors will most likely be able to reach out to a team of experts they work with to help you, including a tax adviser or CPA and a tax attorney, should the need for trust planning arise.

A big part of any person's tax strategy should be the use of tax-advantaged savings plans. These plans may range from IRAs to 401(k)s, 403(b)s or self-employed retirement accounts. What you need to know is there is a tax benefit associated with saving in these types of accounts. I'll explain the various types of retirement accounts, the tax benefits, contribution limits and the characteristics and intricacies of each.

THE POWER OF TAX DEFERRAL.

It can be difficult to determine how much money you'll need for the future. And coming up short is not an option you want to think about. Adding a tax-deferred investment to your portfolio may help you create more retirement income.

In this example, we see the difference between a 30-year old investor paying taxes now versus later.

Considerations when taxes are paid each year:

- 75% of annual earnings are kept
- This may be a better option if the tax rate is expected to increase in the future

Initial investment
$100,000
This example assumes an annual rate of return of 5% and an income tax rate of 25%

After 30 years, the taxable investment grows to: **$301,747**

After 30 years, if a full distribution is taken, the value after taxes will be: **$349,146**

Considerations when taxes are paid later:

- 100% of annual earnings may have the potential to keep growing — offering tax-deffered compound growth
- Ordinary income taxes will need to be paid when distributors are received from the tax-deferred investment
- Tax-deferred investing may be attractive if the future personal income tax rates are expected to decrease

Individual Retirement Account

First, let's discuss the individual retirement account, or IRA. Many people don't realize there are different types of IRAs, so it's important to distinguish the difference. A financial advisor can review these options with you to determine which type of IRA may be more beneficial to your individual circumstances.

Basically, An IRA is an individual retirement account set up at a financial institution that allows an individual to save for retirement on a tax-deferred earnings basis. The three main types of IRAs each have different advantages:

- *Traditional IRA* – You make contributions with money you may be able to deduct on your current year tax return, and any earnings can potentially grow tax-deferred until you withdraw them in retirement. Many retirees may find themselves in a lower tax bracket than they were in prior to retirement, so the tax deferral could mean these funds may be taxed at a lower rate. The maximum allowable contribution for the 2016 tax year is $5,500; however, for those individuals age 50 or older, the limit is $6,500 due to the allowable "catch-up" provision. There are income phaseouts for being able to tax-deduct contributions, as well as early withdrawal penalties imposed by the IRS, so be certain to consult your tax advisor prior to contributing or withdrawing funds from an IRA.
- *Roth IRA* – You make contributions with money you've already paid taxes on (after-tax), and your money may potentially grow tax free, with tax-free withdrawals in retirement, provided that certain conditions are met. The contribution limits are the same as traditional IRAs, however the income phaseout limits are much higher for Roth IRA eligibility.
- *Rollover IRA* – This is a traditional IRA intended for money "rolled over" from a qualified retirement plan. Rollovers involve moving eligible assets from an employer-sponsored plan,

such as a 401(k) or 403(b), into an IRA. The primary benefit of an IRA rollover is it allows the investor the ability to control their own account, including the investment choices offered and investment decisions made within their own account. A rollover IRA also allows the owner to consolidate other IRAs and previous employer retirement plans they participated in, making it easier to manage than having multiple accounts. This should make it less complex when required minimum distributions, or RMDs, start, while reducing the risk of not withdrawing the correct IRS required amounts after age 70 ½, which may lead to a 50% tax penalty being imposed on the withdrawal shortage amount.

- *myRA* – This is not a "true" IRA. This is a plan made available by the U.S. government for people who don't have access to a retirement savings plan at work. It has no fees and goes with you when you change jobs.

All the funds in traditional IRA accounts are subject to ordinary income tax when withdrawn, and, as mentioned above, you are subject to RMDs after age 70 ½. It may be more beneficial to someone who needs more future retirement income to consider a Roth IRA. They forgo a possible current year tax deduction when contributions are made into the account, but when making withdrawals in retirement the proceeds are tax free, subject to certain conditions being met, and are not subject to RMDs. That means you have more control over the timing of your withdrawals. Once again, your tax advisor should discuss the various pros and cons of these plans and determine which may be more beneficial to you.

401(k) Plan

As I wrote earlier in this book, the traditional pension plans that our mothers and fathers had, for the most part, are no longer on the table. Back then, they knew they would get a set amount of money every month for the rest of their lives.

Today, according to the Bureau of Labor Statistics, only 18 percent of full-time American workers have a pension. That's down from 35 percent in just 1990.

The pension has been largely replaced by the 401(k) as companies tire of the expenses and challenges of providing pensions for their workers. What that means for you is that the burden of providing for your future and your retirement rests mainly upon you. With a 401(k) plan, you have to fund the majority of your retirement, you have to choose from the available funds offered by your plan where your money will be invested, and you have to make sure it is correctly allocated among the right investment options based upon factors such as your age, investment objective and risk-tolerance level.

So, why should you invest in a 401(k)? Well, like the IRA, you invest in a 401(k) for the tax deduction and retirement accumulation features. 401(k) contributions are deducted from your paycheck on a pre-tax basis, effectively lowering the amount of income you are taxed on. And, the investments grow without being taxed until you make withdrawals during retirement. If your effective tax rate is less in retirement than during your working years, you'll pay a smaller amount of tax on withdrawals.

Increasingly, employers are offering a Roth option. The Roth 401(k) doesn't give you an immediate tax break. You must pay taxes on any income you contribute to the plan. But you won't have to pay tax on the withdrawals you take in retirement.

As with Roth IRAs, withdrawals from a Roth 401(k) are tax- and penalty-free, as long as you've had the account for five years or longer and are at least age 59 ½ when you take withdrawals. There are no income limits on Roth 401(k) contributions like there are with the Roth IRA, so it's a way for high-wage earners to invest without having to possibly convert a traditional IRA to a Roth IRA for future tax-free income.

It is important that whatever you've already invested in an IRA or 401(k) plan be properly reviewed and properly diversified. It is also important that you understand your plan and how it works, which many people don't. That includes any employer-matching contributions, where available. I would also say with confidence that many people leave those matching employer contributions on the table by not contributing enough themselves to qualify.

Through the years, I've met with hundreds of people who were not taking full advantage of their 401(k), either by not meeting a minimum to qualify for their company's match, or by not contributing as much as they were legally allowed to on a pre-tax basis.

Most of the time, they'll heed my advice by making the necessary changes, and in many cases they weren't even aware of exactly how their plan worked. At the time they enrolled into their employer-sponsored retirement plan, a packet of information was given to them and decisions expected to be made within limited timeframes. They may not understand the intricacies of the plan nor the profound effect it's likely to have on their future retirement lifestyle. When meeting with new clients, I'll always ask them what amount of their retirement plan contributions receive company matching, and inevitably they'll give me that deer-in-the-headlights look. They know they are putting money away for retirement, they just don't have a clue how the employer match works. Most Americans are not financially savvy, especially when it comes to their 401(k) or other type of employer-sponsored plans. Obviously, the earlier you start and the more you contribute to your plan, the better, since you'll have more time to accumulate retirement funds and additional dollars contributed by your employer as well as yourself.

Over the past 30-plus years, I've seen generous companies provide dollar-for-dollar matching of up to 6 or 7 percent of an employee's contribution. That means that for every dollar you put into your 401(k), your company is also contributing the same amount into your account, up to the matching limit.

Then you look at what someone is having deducted from their paycheck, and you see they are only putting in 3 percent. They are potentially leaving a lot of money on the table by not putting in the maximum amount, or at least the amount required for them to qualify for 100 percent of the company's matching contributions.

Let's see if this example hits home. Your annual salary is $75,000. You only put 3 percent of your salary, or $187.50 a month, into your 401(k). Over 30 years at a 4 percent return, that amounts to $126,499.

Now, let's add your company match, which is 3 percent because you only chose to put in 3 percent. That means your $187.50, plus your company's putting in the same amount, for a total of $375 per month. Over 30 years at 4 percent return, you now have $253,000.

Alternately, let's say you contribute 6 percent of your salary, or $375 a month, and your company matches that 6 percent. So, you now have a total of $750 going into your 401(k) each month. Over 30 years, with a minimal 4 percent return, you have $507,196 when you retire. Wow, what a difference!

What I explain to people is that every dollar your employer matches is a 100 percent return. You put a dollar in, they put a dollar in. You have a 100 percent return before you've even invested that money. In these rough economic times, we can't afford not taking full advantage of free matching contributions, wouldn't you agree?

I would also stress that for those people who don't have enough money saved for the type of retirement they want, the age they want to retire and the income they will require, it is absolutely imperative to try contributing the maximum allowable amount into your 401(k), which is now $18,000 for the current tax year for workers under age 50, and $24,000 for those age 50 and older.

That can make an enormous difference to your future retirement income, even if it's only for four or five years.

A lot of people who haven't saved enough just throw their hands up in the air and give up, but they shouldn't. Let me explain why it's almost never too late to start saving.

Most people in that critical five-year period before they retire are also in their peak earnings years. The kids are gone and debt is usually lower. The majority of these people are in a positon where they can actually start saving a lot more than they have in the past. It provides them a current year tax deduction as well, if using the retirement vehicles discussed in this chapter. I have provided 401(k) and other retirement plan review services to many individuals and families throughout my career, and continue to do so today.

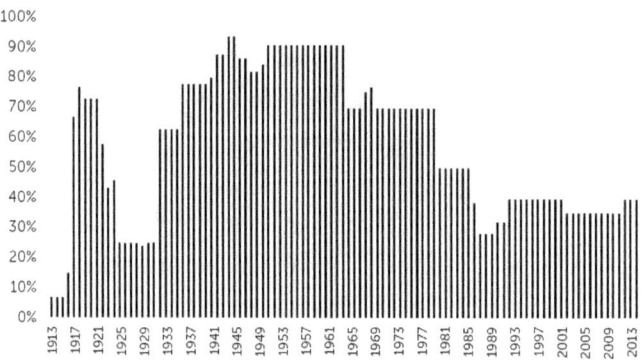

A BRIEF HISTORY OF TAX RATES
TOP MARGINAL TAX RATES

Source: Eugene Steuefle, The Urban Institute; Joseph Pechman, Federal Tax Policy; Joint Committee on Taxation, Summary of Conference Agreement on the Jobs and Growth Tax Relief Reconciliation Act of 2003, JCX-54-03, May 22, 2003; IRS Revised Tax Rate Schedules.

Other Tax-Advantaged Ways to Invest:

403(b) Plan

A 403(b) plan is basically a tax-advantaged retirement savings plan similar to a 401(k), but it's available for only some public universities, hospital service organizations and nonprofit organizations.

457 Plan

The 457 plan is a type of nonqualified, tax-advantaged, deferred-compensation retirement plan that is available for governmental and certain non-governmental employers in the United States. For the most part, these plans operate similarly to 401(k) or 403(b) plans.

Life Insurance

There are many different types of life insurance policies available to consumers, the most common being term, whole life and universal life. Premiums are generally funded using after-tax dollars, however, with permanent cash value type policies, funds accumulate on a tax-deferred basis. Tax-free principal withdrawals and tax-free loans can be utilized to provide additional retirement income. The death benefit is tax free to your beneficiary, and as we discussed in earlier chapters, this may allow your surviving spouse to live a more comfortable retirement lifestyle.

Annuity

Your investment gains accumulate tax deferred. There are different types of annuities.

- Fixed annuities are issued by insurance companies and provide you with a set interest-rate return.

- Variable annuities allow you to invest in different areas of stock markets and bond markets through sub-accounts for potential accumulation.
- The newest hybrid type of annuity, fixed index annuities, provide principle guarantees while allowing you to take positions in various market indexes for potential future growth. Any growth earned is then added to your initial investment amount and also becomes protected against loss.

TAX DEFERRED ANNUITIES
FIXED INDEX ANNUITIES
PRINCIPAL PROTECTED FROM STOCK MARKET LOSSES

- **INDEXED INTEREST POTENTIAL** – opportunity to accumulate interest based on changes in one or more external market indexes; such as the S&P 500, Nasdaq 100, Dow, Bonds and Treasuries, International indexes, Alternative indexes (commodities, currencies, energy) etc. You are not directly invested in a market or index.

- **ANNUAL RESET** – ending value of the index becomes the starting value of the index for the next contract year.

Guarantees and protections provided by annuities are backed by the financial strength and claims paying ability of the issuing insurance carrier.

Although an external index may affect contract values, the contract does not directly participate in any stock, bond or investments.

Retirement annuities can also be designated to provide a guaranteed income for life, regardless of how long someone lives, eliminating longevity risk. We'll go into more specific details on annuities and life insurance in a later chapter.

For the Self-Employed

For those of you who may be self-employed, or running your own businesses, there are various types of plans approved by the tax code that can be implemented to assist you with retirement, which would include defined-contribution pension plans and target-benefit pension plans, which can be highly weighted toward older business owners.

- **Solo 401(k)** – Also known as a self-employed 401(k) or individual 401(k), it is a qualified retirement plan designed specifically for employers with no full-time employees other than the business owner(s) and their spouse(s).
- **SEP IRA** – A provision that allows an employer (typically a small business or self-employed individual) to make retirement plan contributions into a traditional IRA.
- **Simple IRA** – (Savings Incentive Match Plan for Employees of Small Employers) For self-employed people with under 100 employees. You can also have a SIMPLE IRA if you have no employees. If you do have employees, you generally must match up to 3% of their compensation. The plan is similar to a 401(k) plan, but with lower contribution limits and simpler (and thus less costly) administration. Although it is termed an IRA, it is treated separately.

Also, profit-sharing plans allow you to make discretionary contributions based on how your business does in any given year. Though profit-sharing contributions are discretionary, keep in mind, if you make a contribution on behalf of yourself you are also required in most cases to make the same percentage of income contributions for all other employees. You can't discriminate from a percentage basis. If you decide you won't make contributions at all, you have the right to do that.

There are also various business tax deductions. You really need to consult your tax advisor to take full advantage of them. But it is important to do that. Remember, any of these additional tax deductions creates additional fee dollars that can be invested toward your retirement.

CHAPTER SIX

Protecting What You Have: Risk vs. Reward

Most financial planners will tell you that historically the best investment returns are made in the stock market. The average annualized return for the S&P 500 between 1973 and 2014 was 10 percent. No other traditional investment compares to the returns stocks have provided over the long term.

But, as you know, stock markets have up years and down years, and while a portfolio filled with stocks or mutual funds may be the best investment you can make over the long haul, they also may carry a heavy amount of risk as well. Therefore, as you get nearer to retirement you might want to consider damping down on stocks to reduce your overall portfolio risk.

The thinking is pretty basic here. A 40-year-old has maybe 20 years to make up for those "bad" years in the market. But a 55-year-old who plans to retire at age 62 has only a few years to recover market losses. It gets worse if he or she is forced into an earlier retirement than anticipated.

That's why we have to talk about risk here.

Without getting too technical, modern portfolio theory is essentially an attempt to set up a perfect portfolio, taking into consideration risk and reward. For a broader definition: If you take more risk you have more potential return. If you take less risk, you have less potential return. Your goal should be to achieve a portfolio that maximizes your return while minimizing your risk.

At some point when you exceed the ideal portfolio risk level, the advantage isn't there anymore. You must avoid subjecting your portfolio to excessive market risk and potential loss as you begin to make your plans for retirement, or as you get closer to retirement.

You can help to reduce risk and increase your potential returns with a portfolio that includes asset allocation, principal-protected investments, diversification and asset rebalancing.

When you start to think about retirement, it's definitely the right time to have a complete analysis done on your retirement portfolio. That process is what I call a full, pre-retirement analysis, which includes an investment risk assessment.

Essentially, a risk assessment is like a stress test of someone's current investment portfolio — a financial stress test. For example, what I do for my clients is set aside a full hour or two to re-evaluate their entire portfolio, their retirement goals and their essential and discretionary retirement income needs.

We use computer software that runs various scenarios based on things such as market performance and interest rate changes to see how your portfolio would weather these potential pitfalls.

I would also reiterate that during the review, we must consider how much risk it's worth taking to potentially provide you with additional retirement income and weigh that against potential loss of principle.

When I first meet with prospective clients who are pre-retirees looking for a second opinion, oftentimes the stress test reveals their portfolio to be concentrated in stock positions such as small cap stocks and aggressive growth mutual funds, which can be highly volatile. Perhaps these investments made sense when they were purchased, because at that stage of life they were most likely seeking long-term growth.

However, as you near retirement, you need to consider changing your thought process from growth mode to income mode for your investment portfolio. As much as you may want to keep focusing on growing your investments, you need to begin protecting those very assets that will soon be required to produce dependable income to cover your retirement expenses.

For all new clients, I also perform a complete fee analysis on their current investment portfolio to provide them full disclosure as to the fees they are paying for their investments.

As we talked about in earlier chapters, higher fees can play a very negative role in investment performance, asset protection and the amount of income that can be generated from those investments during retirement.

LESSONS FROM 2008 – WITHDRAWALS

YEAR	BEGINNING BALANCE	S&P 500 ANNUAL PERFORMANCE	GAIN/LOSS	WITHDRAWAL	ENDING BALANCE
2008	$500,000	-38.49%	-$192,450	$25,000	$282,550
2009	$282,550	23.45%	$72,120	$25,000	$322,960
2010	$339,234	12.78%	$48,522	$25,000	$339,234
2011	$339,234	0%	$0	$25,000	$314,234
2012	$314,234	13.41%	$57,421	$25,000	$337,373

Data used to create this chart obtained from:
http://www.davemanuel.com/where-did-the-dija-nasdaq-sp500-trade-on.php
This hypothetical example is for illustrative purposes only, and should not be deemed a representation of past or future results, and is no guarantee of return or future performance. Please note, it is not possible to invest directly into the S&P500, this measure is simply provided as a general guage of overall market performance.

Now I want to show you why that risk analysis is so important. I hate to bring up the 2008 market crisis, but there's an important lesson to be learned from it. The market eventually recovered and provided nice gains for people who did not panic and cash out, as it historically has done for those who could afford to wait for a recovery, and had time to do so.

However, many retirees and people close to retirement were just stuck watching their portfolios get decimated at the worst time possible for them. They were planning on living off those portfolio assets, and many were forced to make withdrawals at or near the bottom of the market. Retirees generally cannot wait for a bear market to recover. That's why the risk analysis is so very important.

Here's an example I like to use to show how difficult it can be to recover from a market loss when you don't have time on your side.

If You Lose	Gain Required To Break Even
5%	5%
10%	11%
15%	20%
25%	33%
30%	43%
35%	54%
40%	67%
45%	82%
50%	100%
75%	300%
90%	900%

Over the last 15 years, the average return of the S&P 500 was 2.27 percent. When you include taxes and inflation, you lost money during that long period of time. If you were unlucky enough to have started investing in 2000 or 2008 into those two bear markets, many investors saw their account values plunge nearly 50 percent.

If you lose 50 percent of the value of your portfolio, you have to earn a 100 percent return on those same assets just to get back to where you were before!

Let me explain. If you have a $1 million portfolio and it drops 50 percent, that means you have $500,000 left. You would need to earn a 100 percent return to get back to $1 million. If you were also retired during that period and withdrawing money for living expenses, you would need an even higher return, or possibly you may never see your account return to its original balance.

Now that we've dealt with the most complicated, and potentially the most important, part of reviewing your portfolio, we need to look at other things we need to consider. All of them are important, and some we deal with in more detail in later chapters.

Inflation

Let's assume you retire at age 65 and start taking $50,000 a year from your portfolio for living expenses. If you assume a 4 percent annual inflation rate, by the time you reach the age of 83, your income needs would have doubled. That highlights the danger of having a retirement income plan that's set up to only provide you with the same annual income each year, one that doesn't take the silent killer, inflation, into account.

And remember, over the past 10 years there have been several years where Social Security benefits did not provide cost-of-living increases (COLA) because the Social Security Administration (SSA) uses certain inflation factors to determine these COLAs.

Retirees should keep this in mind. Generally, your essential expenses in retirement — things like real estate taxes, health insurance, food, utilities, prescription drugs and medical costs — have historically risen much faster than the government-reported inflation rate.

Retirement Budget

That's a perfect segue into the next related, but equally important, subject — a budget.

You can't have a proper retirement plan, especially an income plan, without a budget. Let me put it this way: A financial advisor can't help you reach your goals without knowing where you're starting from.

Most financial planners will ask you to do that budget before they even start on a financial plan. It's that important.

People often think they have a good grasp on what their expenses will be in retirement. My experience is that most of them will be very wrong. After you do the numbers, you'll probably find that your estimates will be off by 30 percent or more.

Yes, I know, most people loathe the idea of preparing a complete budget, but it is essential prior to retirement, and your financial advisor can help make it less painful for you. A retirement budget and income plan comes down to two areas — your essential spending (needs) and your discretionary spending (wants).

Your essential needs are costs associated with such things as housing, utilities, food, health insurance and medical care, transportation. Discretionary income covers all those extras and wants — hobbies, eating out, theater, a second home, vacations, even visiting children and grandchildren who may live far away.

So, how do you get a handle on those costs? Go to your local dollar store (or drugstore or supermarket) and buy a $1 spiral notebook. For the next 30 days, write down everything you spend.

The longer you have patience to write down those expenses, the more accurate the budget will be. That's because you need to allow for one-time shocks to your budget — things like that $300 car repair bill or the $200 in extra groceries you had to buy because your brother, his wife and their three kids came to stay with you for a week.

Your financial advisor will then look at all your expenses, and compare them to all your future retirement income sources — 401(k), pension (if you have one), Social Security, annuities, etc. — to determine if you have a "gap". A budget gap is of course the difference between your income and expenses, and many people fall short. There are ways to fix that gap if you are 10 years away from retirement, or even five years away.

Then we have time to talk about ways to make it up, whether it involves saving more in your retirement accounts or possibly working a year or two longer than anticipated.

The problem comes when you haven't planned ahead and realize a year before you're ready to retire that you have a big budget gap!

In any event, we'll discuss this more in later chapters.

Guaranteed Income

There should also be a discussion of the base or foundation of your future guaranteed retirement income plan. As previously mentioned, back in the day, most companies provided a pension for their employees when they retired. They would provide a set amount of money every month for life.

Now you are more likely to have a 401(k). It's up to you to figure out how to turn those assets into income and make it last throughout your lifetime, and perhaps your spouse's lifetime as well!

Household Monthly Budget

	Budget	Actual	Variance
Income			
Salary 1 Take Home Pay	$3,750.00	$3,750.00	$0.00
Salary 2 Take Home Pay	$2,750.00	$2,750.00	$0.00
(Other Income)	$250.00	$0.00	$250.00
(Other Income)	$0.00	$0.00	$0.00
Total Income	$6,750.00	$6,500.00	$250.00
Expenses			
Fixed Costs			
Mortgage / Rent Expense	$1,000.00	$1,000.00	$0.00
Car Lease Payment(s)	$850.00	$850.00	$0.00
Loan Payment(s)	$350.00	$350.00	$0.00
Insurance - Car	$100.00	$100.00	$0.00
Insurance - Homeowners	$75.00	$75.00	$0.00
Insurance - Life	$75.00	$75.00	$0.00
Charitable Contributions	$200.00	$200.00	$0.00
Childcare	$1,000.00	$1,000.00	$0.00
(Other Fixed Costs)	$0.00	$0.00	$0.00
(Other Fixed Costs)	$0.00	$0.00	$0.00
Total Fixed Costs	$3,650.00	$3,650.00	$0.00
Semi-Variable Costs			
Electric / Gas Expense	$400.00	$375.00	$25.00
Telephone Expense	$75.00	$75.55	-$0.45
Cable / Satellite Television Exp	$100.00	$105.25	-$5.25
Internet Expense	$75.00	$76.00	-$1.00
Food / Dining Out & Groceries	$750.00	$770.55	-$20.55
Gasoline	$400.00	$384.00	$16.00
Pet Supplies	$80.00	$66.54	$13.46
Medical / Healthcare	$75.00	$104.25	-$29.25
Personal Care	$75.00	$70.59	$4.41
(Other Semi-Variable Costs)	$0.00	$0.00	$0.00
(Other Semi-Variable Costs)	$0.00	$0.00	$0.00
Total Semi-Variable Costs	$2,000.00	$2,027.73	$2.00
Highly Variable Costs			
Entertainment	$150.00	$204.55	-$54.55
Gifts	$50.00	$42.55	$7.47
Clothing	$150.00	$175.55	-$25.55
Miscellaneous	$100.00	$105.00	-$5.00

We know a solid foundation of any retirement income plan is Social Security, though some might argue the merits of relying on a government program that always seems to be in fiscal trouble. We also know Social Security should not be relied upon as the only source of retirement income, nor was it designed to be. Therefore, you must also look at other guaranteed income sources. If you don't have a pension or other reliable, guaranteed income sources, you should probably consider some type of retirement annuity.

I've met with hundreds of people through the years who come to me for a review of their portfolio statements, oftentimes right before they retire. Many are shocked after we perform the financial stress test to learn the amount of risk they are carrying in their current portfolio. That is not good at a time when most are trying to protect their principle and their future income against loss.

With that in mind, I often discuss with them how the only investment vehicle that can provide them and their spouse with guaranteed income for life, regardless of how long they may live, is an annuity.

Most pre-retirees that I've met with have a few simple goals — not losing principal, keeping growth potential and guaranteeing a certain amount of inflation-adjusted income for life for themselves and their spouse.

If that's the case, I will often recommend fixed index annuities, which, as discussed before, are contracts with an insurance company. For a lump sum investment, the insurance company guarantees you a certain amount of income for the rest of your life (and your spouse's, if you choose a joint payout).

Fixed index annuities offer growth potential based on returns of various market indexes offered within the annuity.

Some insurance companies offer uncapped indexes, meaning you fully participate in any upside of the index, less a preset margin retained by the company. Say the index you're participating in returns 10 percent during the participation period. You would receive this 10 percent return, minus the preset margin, let's say 1.5 percent. This would result in an 8.5 percent net rate of return for that period of time. This "interest credit" would then be added to your principal amount and become protected against loss.

Fixed index annuities differ in many ways from variable annuities. Many fixed index annuities are offered with no annual fees, other than for additional riders you may choose to add on, whereas a typical variable annuity charges an annual mortality and expense (M&E) fee, sub-account management fees and rider fees. These fees, which can be quite large, are deducted directly from your account balance. Variable annuities generally do not offer principal protection, which also means you are taking 100 percent of the risk. If your sub-account fund goes down say, 40 percent, you suffer the entire loss. With fixed index annuities, if the return of the index you're invested in is negative, your return for that period is zero. In a bear market, zero is our hero.

The reason fixed index annuity sales are growing so rapidly, especially in the pre-retiree market, is the safety they provide by offering upside potential with zero downside risk to your principal. Most of you probably know who Tony Robbins is. He is a nationally known motivational speaker and self-help author. In his recent book, "Money, Master the Game," he interviews some of the most famous investors in the world — such as Warren Buffet, Sir John Templeton or John Bogle of Vanguard funds — to find out how they manage their assets. Tony makes a profound comment that fixed index annuities may be the greatest investment available on the planet, due to their principal protection, low-fee structure (in some cases no fees), potential for growth and guaranteed income for life!

In his book, he also refers to a hybrid fixed index annuity that offers both a fixed rate of return and an option of a return tied to the growth of various market indexes. These offer 100 percent guarantee of your principal as well, and any interest credited to your account is added to your protected principal. That means that not only is it principal-protected, but it is growth-protected, as well.

We will more fully review the benefits and challenges of various types of annuities in the next chapter.

CHAPTER SEVEN

Understanding Annuities 101

What are people worried about when it comes to retirement? According to a survey by Allianz, they are mostly afraid of outliving their savings.

According to the Allianz survey, 61 percent of the survey takers said they were more scared of outliving their savings than they were of dying. That number rose to 77 percent for those aged 44 to 49, and 82 percent for people their late 40s with dependents.

There is good reason for those concerns. Most Americans have not saved enough for retirement and we are living longer.

Incredibly, 31 percent of Americans have saved nothing for retirement, and that includes 19 percent of Americans between the ages of 55 and 64, according to the Federal Reserve Board.

Add to that our longer life expectancies. Today, the average 65-year-old couple has a 52 percent chance that at least one spouse will reach the age of 95.

THE RETIREMENT DILEMMA

As you plan for retirement, you will likely encounter some challenges. It helps to be aware of the hurdles you may face.

Longer life expectancies

Today's longer life expectancies mean you will likely spend more years in retirement. Planning how you will fund those extra years takes on added importance.

Today, the average 65-year-old couple has a 52% chance that at least one spouse will reach the age of 95[1].

Probability of living from 65 to various ages[1]

	65	80	85	90	95	100
♂		82%	69%	50%	27%	9%
♀		85%	75%	57%	35%	14%
♂♀		97%	92%	79%	52%	22%

A shift in responsibility

While pensions were once a reliable source of retirement income, the burden of funding retirement has shifted overwhelmingly to the individual. Regardless of whether you choose to fund your retirement years through a 401(k) or with other investments, you will most likely need to take a more active role in your retirement planning.

Sources of retirement income

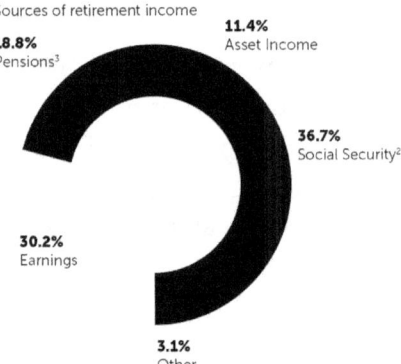

- 18.8% Pensions[3]
- 11.4% Asset Income
- 36.7% Social Security[2]
- 3.1% Other
- 30.2% Earnings

[1] Based on the Annuity 2012 Generational Mortality Table.
[2] Income of the Aged Chartbook, 2010 Social Security Administration, Office of Research, Evaluation and Statistics (October 2010).
[3] Pensions include defined benefit and defined contribution plans.

That brings us back to our discussion of how, if you don't have a financial advisor, you are literally on your own when you are planning for retirement.

We certainly can't depend on our company-sponsored pensions anymore. Only 18 percent of full-time workers in America still have pensions. Still, retirees will find that it is imperative that they have some sort of guaranteed income. Most will find that Social Security alone just won't cut it — not if they want to maintain the lifestyles they have grown accustomed to. The Social Security Administration says that the average monthly Social Security payment to retired workers will be $1,341 in 2016.

And that brings us to our discussion of annuities.

There is no doubt about it — annuities over the years have garnered a pretty bad reputation. They have been portrayed by much of the press as fee-laden investments pushed by bad or rogue commission brokers and insurance agents more interested in high commissions than in helping their clients.

Sure, while there may be some truth in that, as I said earlier, there have always been bad brokers and there always will be, just like there are some bad doctors and bad lawyers.

But the majority of financial advisors are good, hard-working people trying to use their skills to help their clients achieve a certain quality of life in retirement.

It seems the tide is turning much more favorably on the way the financial press reports on annuities, largely due to the realization of the importance annuities can play in a sound retirement income plan. What has also changed dramatically is the number of new choices available when it comes to annuities. Most every financial advisor I know now recommends that annuities be a part of your income plan in retirement. They are no longer just an option or afterthought, because so few people have traditional pensions these days, they have become a necessary cog for any successful retirement income strategy.

Today, annuities factor in a great many retirement plans because they are virtually the only investment available on the planet that guarantees a lifetime income for you, and possibly your spouse, regardless of how long you live. That eliminates the longevity risk we all face, which we talked about earlier in this chapter. As you saw in the large-scale Allianz study, people are extremely worried they will outlive their money and face the choice of either having to go back to work or live as paupers.

A successful retirement plan has to include income that is guaranteed every month regardless of how the stock or bond markets may be performing.

Because of the bad press in the past, sometimes I see the doubt in a client's eyes when I mention the dreaded "A" word (annuities). When I get that initial reaction, I ask them what investment vehicle they think traditional pensions and lotteries use? They buy an immediate annuity that will guarantee that person a certain amount of money every month for life!

During one's asset-accumulation stage of life, stocks and mutual funds may be highly appropriate and provide the potential growth an investor desires. During one's retirement-income stage, however, it's a little impractical to sell off small portions of stocks or mutual funds to provide the monthly income a retiree needs to pay expenses. In addition, as we have discussed in detail, this would also leave a retiree with no practical way of determining how long his or her assets may last, since that would largely depend on unknown future market returns.

So, before we go any further, I'd like to offer you a glossary of terms to help you understand annuities, courtesy of the Indexed Annuity Leadership Council (IALC) in Washington, D.C.

- Annuity: A contract in which an insurance company makes a series of income payments at regular intervals in return for a premium or premiums you have paid. Annuities are often bought for future retirement income. Only an annuity can pay an income that can be guaranteed to last as long as you live. Your money grows tax deferred as long as you leave it in the annuity.

- Annuitant: The person who receives the benefits of an annuity.
- Compounding interest: Interest paid both on the original amount of money and on the interest it has already earned.
- Simple interest: Interest paid based only on the original amount of money and not on the interest it has already earned.
- Defined-benefit plans: A type of pension plan in which an employer/sponsor promises a specified monthly benefit on retirement that is predetermined by a formula based on the employee's earnings history, tenure of service and age, rather than depending directly on individual investment returns. The plan provides lifetime income through a group or individual annuity contract.
- Fixed annuity: An insurance contract in which the insurance company makes fixed dollar payments to the annuitant for the term of the contract, usually until the annuitant dies. The insurance company guarantees both earnings and principal.
- Fixed indexed annuity (FIA): A fixed annuity on which credited interest is based upon the performance of an index, such as the S&P 500. The principal is protected from losses in the equity market, while gains add to the annuity's returns. Interest credited is not based on pre-declared rates of interest typical of traditional fixed annuities.
- Guaranteed lifetime withdrawal benefit (GLWB)/income rider: An optional benefit that can be attached to an annuity contract for an additional cost that will provide a lifetime income stream that can be turned on in the future. Some income riders grow at a contractually guaranteed rate that will compound during the deferral years for future lifetime income.

- Guarantee period: An option to ensure that a minimum number of years' payments are made by the annuity, even if you die. The maximum guarantee period is normally 30 years. If you die during the guarantee period, the annuity will continue to make income payments to the named beneficiary until the end of the selected guarantee period, or you could select that the remaining payments be paid out as a lump sum (this option is not permitted under certain circumstances).
- Immediate annuity: An annuity purchased with a single premium on which income payments begin within one year of the contract date. With fixed immediate annuities, the payment is based on a specified interest rate. With variable immediate annuities, payments are based on the value of the underlying investments. Payments are made for the life of the annuitant(s), for a specified period, or both (e.g., 10 years certain and life).
- Longevity risk: The risk of outliving one's assets.
- Lump-sum distribution: The distribution at retirement of a participant's entire account balance within one calendar year due to retirement, death or disability.
- Lump-sum option: A withdrawal option in which the annuity is surrendered and all assets are withdrawn in a single payment.
- Principal: An amount of money that is loaned, borrowed or invested, apart from any additional money such as interest.
- Purchase price: The amount that is used to buy the annuity.
- Refinancing: Revising a payment schedule, usually to reduce monthly payments. A common reason to do this is to reduce the interest rate on a mortgage.
- Surrender charge: A type of sales charge imposed if you surrender your annuity or withdraw amounts over and above the contractually allowed withdrawal percentage (usually 10 percent annually) from an annuity during the "surrender period"

- a set period of time that typically lasts seven to 10 years after you purchase the annuity.
- Tax deferred: An investment that accumulates earnings that are not subject to current taxation until the investor takes possession of the earnings by way of withdrawal.
- Variable annuity: An insurance company contract into which the buyer makes a lump-sum payment or series of payments. In return, the insurer agrees to make periodic payments beginning immediately or at some future date. Purchase payments are directed to a range of investment options referred to as sub-accounts, or directly into the separate account of the insurance company that manages the portfolios. The value of the account during accumulation, and the income payments after annuitization (maturity) vary, depending on the performance of the investment options chosen.
- Vesting: Reaching the point, through length of service, at which an employee acquires the right to receive employer-contributed benefits, such as pensions or defined-contribution employer-matched dollars.

If someone were to say "I don't like stocks," you would have to reply "Which ones don't you like?" since there are more than 15,000 different stocks currently trading on various markets. Just as you can't lump all stocks or all bonds together as one, there are many different types of annuities, some of which we touched on in this and previous chapters. Annuities can and do play a key role in many different situations, as already discussed. Let me share just one of these with you now. An anesthesiologist from Buffalo, New York, was referred to me by an existing client of mine from the same area about 20 years ago. This doctor was a stock jockey. He only liked to buy individual stocks, either ones that he chose or ones his colleagues suggested he buy. By his own admission, his portfolio was always up and down.

For years, I would meet with him occasionally and suggest that perhaps he should consider an annuity as a safer alternative for some of his retirement money, since the market roller coaster concerned him. I could never get him to take my advice and make a change. He had an intense dislike for annuities and would always cite the bad press they received.

After the market crash of 2000 to 2002, as despondent as he was, he continued with the same attitude. He thought things would get better — the market would bounce back. Sure enough, he was right. From 2003 to 2007, the stock market had a big recovery. But I correctly pointed out to him that he still had no growth in his portfolio. In fact, he was merely back to where he started 10 years ago. Measured against inflation, he was actually losing money!

Then, along came the massive financial crisis beginning in late 2007 when Lehman Brothers failed and the government began the bailout of many large institutions like AIG and General Motors. The stock market plunged like never before and, during a relatively short period of time, we saw the S&P 500 drop a record 57 percent through March of 2009.

Likewise, my doctor friend saw his portfolio once again drop another 50 percent. Finally, when I went to visit him right after that, he said "I can't keep going through this or I'll never be able to retire ... Every time my investment portfolio recovers we go into another bear market again."

So, we sat down in his home for a three-hour meeting. We discussed his future retirement income needs, and we discussed annuities.

UNITED STATES BEAR MARKET OF 2007 – 2009

DATE	NASDAQ	% CHANGE	S&P 500	% CHANGE	DOW JONES	% CHANGE	NOTES
JANUARY 3, 2007	2423.16	—	1416.60	—	12,474.52	—	
OCTOBER 9, 2007	2803.91	+15.71%	1565.15	+10.49%	14,164.53	+13.55%	THE DAY THE DJIA AND S&P 500 PEAKED
OCTOBER 10, 2007	2811.61	+0.27%	1562.47	-0.17%	14,078.69	-0.61%	THE DAY THE NASDAQ PEAKED
JANUARY 2, 2008	2609.63	-7.18%	1447.16	-7.38%	13,043.96	-7.35%	
JUNE 27, 2008	2315.63	-11.27%	1278.38	-11.66%	11,346.51	-13.01%	THE DAY AFTER THE BEAR MARKET DECLARED
NOVEMBER 4, 2008	1780.12	-23.13%	1005.75	-21.33%	9,625.28	-15.17%	ELECTION DAY
JANUARY 2, 2009	1632.21	-8.31%	899.35	-10.58%	9,034.69	-6.14%	
JANUARY 20, 2009	1440.86	-11.72%	804.47	-10.55%	7949.09	-12.02%	INAUGURATION OF BARACK OBAMA
MARCH 9, 2009	1268.64	-11.95%	676.53	-15.90%	6507.04	-18.14%	THE DAY THE DJIA, S&P 500 AND NASDAQ BOTTOMED
OCTOBER 9, 2007 TO MARCH 9, 2009	-1543	-54.9%	-886	-56.6%	-7657	-53.9%	CUMMULATIVE CHANGE (FROM PEAK TO BOTTOM)

Source: Wikipedia
http://en.wikipedia.org/wiki/United_States_bear_market_of_2007%E2%80%9309

Finally, he agreed to shift about 50 percent of his assets, most of which were his most volatile, risky assets. We reallocated those risky assets into an annuity with an income benefit rider, which provides a guaranteed minimum determinable future monthly benefit regardless of stock market performance.

He's very happy today. Most times when the market drops precipitously, he'll call me and thank me for making those changes and allowing him to sleep better at night, knowing that the majority of his retirement income is now protected. You would be surprised by the amount of comfort this provides current and future retirees.

There are many similar examples I've had working with clients throughout the years. As we discussed in the last chapter, we've seen that stocks over a long period of time historically outperform other investments. But it's imperative to look at the stage of life you're in now, how close you may be to your retirement date, and to make appropriate adjustments to your portfolio to reduce your risk of principal loss. You can't turn back the clock, as much as we'd like to.

There are many different types of annuities. Just like choosing the right financial advisor is critically important, it's also extremely important to work with an advisor who has a great deal of experience in the area of annuities due to the product's complexities, along with the multitude and types of annuities available in today's marketplace. Today, annuity companies are competing hard for your business by constantly upgrading their offerings. It's all about finding the right insurance company and the right annuity contract for your specific needs. Therefore, it makes perfect sense to work with someone independent who can offer you the best available options, regardless of which insurance company that may be, rather than an agent or broker tied to one insurance company, who can only offer you what that particular company may be selling at any given time.

A COMPELLING CASE FOR ANNUITIES

Not one Fixed Index Annuity owner has ever lost their principal profits from market volatility or insurance company failure. Not one time, **NOT ONE DIME!**

- Traditional market investments don't offer this.
- Banks can't say this.
- Bondholders can't say this.
- Money market owners can't say this.
- Real Estate investors can't say this.
- Precious metal investors can't say this.
- Variable annuity investors can't say this.

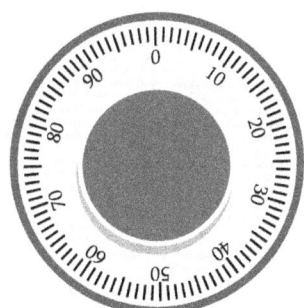

For years, if Americans wanted opportunity, they would put their savings in the stock market. If they wanted safety, they used bank CDs or government bonds. The problem was you could have money positioned for opportunity or safety, but not **both on the same dollar at the same time.**

Today, billions of dollars annually are finding how to have safety and opportunity on the same dollar at the same time. The vehicle that has filled the gap between the stock market and banks is the **Fixed Index Annuity.**

The reason I chose to work with Advisors Excel, which is by far the largest insurance and annuity marketing organization in the country, is they are contracted with nearly 100 different insurance companies, allowing maximum independent choice for our clients. Even within insurance companies themselves, they change products so frequently, and we want the most up-to-date options available at any given time.

By being independent advisors and working with the largest independent marketing agency in the country, we feel strongly that this allows us to serve our clients better, with more available options and better choices. Advisors Excel is so large, in fact, that insurance companies often allow them to completely design the annuity product themselves and offer distribution only to their advisors, like our firm. This often gives us a unique, distinct advantage over other advisors and firms not able to offer their clients the same newly created annuities!

I've been licensed in the insurance and annuity field for 35 years, which I believe provides our clients a tremendous experience advantage over much of the younger generation just trying to break into the financial services industry today.

Do keep in mind, annuities may not be right for everyone, nor every situation. They are meant to be long-term investments, and you may be subjected to early withdrawal penalties by the IRS and the insurance company under certain circumstances.

Since annuities now play such a defining role in most retirement income plans, the financial advisor you choose to work with should possess an in-depth, extensive knowledge of annuities as well as the current annuity marketplace.

An expert annuity advisor like myself will provide full disclosure to you so you are aware of any and all fees and charges, advantages, disadvantages and riders. I like to discuss how I arrive at my conclusion to recommend certain annuities for certain clients, since every situation I encounter and work on is different.

CHAPTER EIGHT

Social Security

Social Security can play a key role in many Americans' retirement income plan, as a foundation block for guaranteed income for life. It can also be a highly emotional and deeply personal decision as to when the best time to begin taking benefits may be for your personal situation.

For a husband and wife approaching retirement, there are hundreds of various options on how and when to begin taking benefits, and with Social Security Administration employees unable by mandate to provide advice to you, it's very important for your financial advisor to help you make the right choices to make sure you aren't potentially leaving tens of thousands of dollars on the table. Just as I advise my clients on their employer-controlled 401(k) plans, though it may not produce income or fees for me, I provide the same service, giving them information that can help them make decisions about their Social Security withdrawal strategies for their specific situations. I include a computer-software-generated optimization report with every retirement income plan my office provides.

The bottom line: I am looking out for the best interests of my clients — as all financial advisors should. There is no way to provide an accurate financial plan or retirement income plan without properly reviewing all aspects of a person's financial life, specifically including their investment portfolio, 401(k) or other retirement plan(s), as well as their Social Security options, thus allowing me to make recommendations based on facts rather than assumptions.

Still, there are many advisors who either don't fully understand Social Security or they prefer to deal only with a person's investments. They may set up an income plan for those investments, but they don't provide any full scale income plan that includes Social Security lifetime benefits. As far as I'm concerned, it's incomplete and misleading if it doesn't include a review of the optimal time and strategy to turn on Social Security benefits, which might mean utilizing other income-producing assets for the first few years of retirement while deferring benefits, thereby allowing future benefits to grow by as much as 8 percent annually up to age 70. A physician would never look at only 50 percent of a patient's medical records to determine the best course of treatment; neither should a financial advisor, that's just common sense!

This has been something I have tried to do for all of my clients since my very first day in the financial services business. It's that important.

As you now know, there are many difficult decisions to be made when you are approaching retirement. Hopefully, you have already made some of the most difficult — choosing the right financial advisor for you, knowing if you will stay in your current home or choose to live elsewhere, when you would like to retire.

But Social Security may be one of the hardest — and most complicated.

That's why it's so important to study and be prepared — and not wait until you are facing a deadline to make your decision. Study your options when you are still in your 50s, and get some professional advice.

There are so many different strategies for different people in different situations that sometimes it may be hard to generalize.

That's the very reason we have invested in computer software to help match our clients' needs with information about Social Security strategies that could fit their situations.

Many financial advisors will automatically recommend that their clients wait until age 70, mostly because they will then get the maximum benefit allowable.

From a personal perspective, I do believe it makes sense to wait as long as possible before you start electing to take your Social Security benefit, however, there are exceptions to this strategy. For instance, what if you are not in the best of health or if your family doesn't have a good history of longevity? If you haven't saved enough and still insist on retiring early, say at age 62, it may be necessary to begin taking Social Security at that time just to make ends meet.

Yet statistically, a majority of people take it earlier — at age 62, in many cases due to a lack of knowledge or proper planning.

But keep this in mind. By waiting just four years to your full retirement age 66, you'll avoid incurring a 25 percent penalty to your monthly check. And if you're able to defer taking benefits until age 70 through proper retirement planning, you'll add another 8 percent to your monthly check for every year that you delay, which is a huge difference!

While many people take benefits early because they need it, others take it for more emotional reasons — they paid into it and they want to get every dime out of it. They may feel that by waiting until age 70, it could take too long for them to break even — to make up for all the benefits they haven't taken since they became eligible. The "break-even" point is age 76 ½, so there are considerations to be made, including one's health, financial well-being and spousal needs at the time. Your financial advisor will guide you through this decision making process.

The average American receives $1,340 a month in benefits, the Social Security Administration says.

As you can see, there is a lot to consider when making this all-important decision.

Longevity should be one of the major considerations. People are routinely living well into their 80s and 90s these days, so taking benefits early could mean shortchanging yourself for years to come.

That means that the average benefit of $1,340 a month could have been $1,688 a month just three years later. And, for most people, there's no turning back after they made the decision to take benefits early. You'll live with that decision for life, and it will also likely affect your spouse's benefits. Once you begin receiving your benefit payment, the clock begins. If you change your mind and want to defer, you must opt to do so within a one-year window, and repay the benefits you've already received.

Again, it is an extremely difficult and complicated decision for many people, but also one of the most important retirement decisions to be made, and it lasts a lifetime. Don't take it lightly or base your decision on what your friend or neighbor chose to do. Your situation is different than theirs and should be treated as such!

Here are some key ages and numbers, all from SocialSecurity.gov.

- **62:** The earliest you can claim Social Security benefits, and the age at which most people take it. Two-thirds of Americans take their benefits as soon as they are eligible. You can choose to receive benefits any time after age 62. But you lock in benefits at 25% less than if you had waited until full retirement age.
- **66:** This is full retirement age for most baby boomers, but it depends on the year in which you were born. Sixty-six is the full retirement age for people born between 1943 and 1954. After that it slowly goes up to 67 (check the SSA website, SocialsSecurity.gov). Only 14% of men and 10% of women wait until age 66, according to the SSA.

- **70:** This is the age at which you receive the maximum benefits allowed. It is also the age many financial planners suggest their clients take Social Security. By waiting, your benefits would increase by approximately 8% a year between 66 and 70. There is no financial incentive to wait beyond age 70 to begin taking benefits. Only 1-2% of Americans wait until 70, and they are usually in the higher-income group, according to the SSA.

Although the SSA website, SocialSecurity.gov, is an excellent source of information, and is really a good way to check on your benefits and even to apply for benefits, it will not advise you on the best claiming strategy for you and your situation. SSA employees are also mandated not to provide advice to individuals on when to begin taking benefits, or what strategies may work best in any individual case.

When and how you claim Social Security is an integral part of any successful income strategy for retirement. However, if you are still seeking additional information before committing to working with an advisor, here is a list of some of the best Social Security guides available.

Books

1. **"Get What's Yours: The 'Revised' Secrets to Maxing Out Your Social Security,"** by Laurence J. Kotlikoff, Philip Moeller and Paul Solman, Simon and Shuster, $12.35 Amazon, $11.99 Kindle edition.

    This New York Times best-seller was updated in 2016 with the new rules, especially the abolition of the "file and suspend" strategy popular with high-income couples by Congress. As its popularity indicates, it's an easy read and an excellent resource. And it answers very question you could possibly have about Social Security. Some especially

insightful chapters: "Be Careful Taking Social Security's Advice and Help," and "Three General Rules to Maximize Your Lifetime Benefits."
2. **"Social Security for Dummies,"** hardback, second edition, Jonathan Peterson, AARP, $39.99, paperback, $10.55, Kindle edition, $10.02.

   Highlights: Easy explanations of Social Security's complex rules; how to use Social Security calculators and statements; advice on when to start collecting retirement benefits; ways to keep your Social Security number safe from theft; how to help a loved one apply for and manage benefits; when and how to handle benefit mistakes and disputes; myths about Social Security.
3. **"The Social Security Claiming Guide: A guide to the most important financial decision you'll likely make,"** 2016 edition, $1.50, by Steven Sass, Alicia H. Munnell, and Andrew Eschtruth, Center for Retirement Research at Boston College.

   If you're approaching retirement, when you claim benefits is one of the most important financial decision you'll likely make. *"The Social Security Claiming Guide"* sorts through all the options, spells out how much you can get, and answers frequently asked questions — all in a clear, easy-to-read and colorful format.
4. **"Maximizing Your Social Security Retirement Benefits,"** Mary Beth Franklin, contributing editor, Investment News, $29.95. Also available as a PDF download at *InvestmentNews* online.
5. **"Guide to Social Security,"** 44th edition, Donna A. Clements, B.A. Manager, Social Security Information Services, Mercer, 400 West Market Street, Suite 700 Louisville, Kentucky 40202-3346. www.imercer.com/socialsecurity. Free.

The dream of a financially secure retirement starts with knowing what benefits Social Security will provide — over 50% of many retirees' income. The "2016 Guide to Social Security" is the perfect resource to give out to explain Social Security and how to get the most out of these benefits.

Available at SocialSecurity.gov

- **"What You Need to Know When You Get Retirement or Survivors Benefits,"** available in audio or PDF, under Retirement Publications, March 2016.
Find out what you can expect from Social Security, what your reporting responsibilities are and how to report changes that could affect benefits.
- **"Benefits for Children,"** available in audio or PDF, under Retirement Publications, March 2016. Many children are eligible for benefits because one or both of their parents are disabled, retired or deceased.
- **"How Work Affects Your Benefits,"** available in audio or PDF, under Retirement Publications, January 2016. Find out how working after beginning to receive retirement benefits can lead to increases or decreases in benefits.
- **"Your Retirement Benefit: How It Is Figured,"** available in audio or PDF, under Retirement Publications, January 2016. Learn about the formula used to calculate Social Security retirement benefits and take advantage of a worksheet to help you estimate your retirement benefits.

Using all available resources to make the right decision when to begin taking your benefits can make a huge difference in your retirement standard of living.

CHAPTER NINE

Rollovers: It's Your Money, Take It With You

With the loss of traditional pension plans for most American workers, tax-advantaged 401(k) plans have provided millions of Americans with the primary means to save for retirement.

But, as I've said in earlier chapters, the shift of American workers relying primarily on pensions to relying on employer-sponsored contribution plans has been somewhat problematic. We're at the point where some are actually calling 401(k) plans an outright failure.

Clearly, the responsibility for making the right investment decisions has been shifted from the company to the worker. And, starting with the decision to actually save — or save *enough* — money, Americans have faltered a great deal in that decision making.

I hear all the time from clients that their companies' human resource departments offer little or no advice or guidance when it comes to 401(k) plans. That goes for how much to save each pay period, which funds to invest in and how to figure out how much retirement income you may actually need.

We've discussed much of that already. In this chapter, I'd like to focus on the people who have saved in their 401(k) plans. I'd like to answer a question I get from clients and potential clients all the time: When I leave my job (or retire), should I leave my 401(k) where it is, transfer it to my new company's plan or roll over my funds to an IRA?

My answer is unequivocal: Effect a qualified rollover to your own IRA account! Do not leave it with a company you have otherwise cut ties with. Take your money with you when you leave. Many advisors suggest you complete the paperwork by your last day of work, to begin the process of rolling over your 401(k) or other retirement account to an IRA, and I completely agree. That way, you insure that it's completed promptly.

It is, after all, *your* money.

There is certainly a lot at stake.

According to the Investment Company Institute, 401(k) plans held an estimated $4.4 trillion in assets in 2014 and represented nearly 18 percent of the $24.0 trillion in U.S. retirement assets. Nearly 65 percent of 401(k) assets were held in mutual funds.

As for 401(k) account balances, they tended to be higher the longer 401(k) plan participants had been working for their current employers and the older the participant was. According to ICI and the Employee Benefits Research Institute, participants in their 60s with more than 30 years of tenure at their current employer had an average 401(k) account balance of $224,287 in 2012. Participants in their 40s with more than five to 10 years of tenure at their current employer had an average 401(k) balance of $53,060. The median 401(k) plan participant was 45 years old, and the median job tenure was eight years.

Meanwhile, baby boomers are retiring at a rate of 10,000 a day. In 2014, an estimated $325 billion was withdrawn from 401(k) plans as boomers retired. Those withdrawals are projected to reach $500 billion in a few years, according to Cerulli & Associates, a Boston research firm.

Frankly, in my opinion, as well as what I've witnessed in reviewing 401(k) assets, the majority of workers have fallen tremendously short of what they will require to enjoy the quality of life they desire in retirement! While there are few to no good reasons to ever leave your 401(k) or other retirement plan assets with your previous employer's plan, there are many very good reasons not to.

Increase Your Options

Why do I say that? It's pretty simple. For companies offering a 401(k) plan to their employees, they are merely required to offer a certain number of different kinds of investment options within the plan, usually mutual funds — a cash option, a fixed option, a bond option and a stock option. They may also offer balanced target date funds as well, which invest based upon a person's age and years until expected retirement, but that's essentially it.

There are reasons your company may only offer a limited number of funds in your retirement plan. Typically, the more fund options they offer in their 401(k), the higher the administration fees they pay will be. If you have 30 funds as opposed to, say, only eight funds, whoever is administering the plan will likely charge higher fees to maintain the plan. Throughout my career, I've witnessed many employers choosing plans based on simplicity, cost savings and other reasons not directly based on what's in the best interest of their employees.

While employers are required to offer a range of different funds within their 401(k) plan, including various risk levels, most often your choices will end up being somewhat limited due to cost or administrative reasons. By rolling over your 401(k) or other retirement plan assets to your own personal IRA right after a separation of service, you open up a world of possible investment options to choose from. As most of us have learned during our lifetime, it usually holds true that the more choices we have, the better the results tend to be!

Don't get me wrong, in today's world the 401(k) is the predominant way for Americans to save for their retirement, and I always encourage people to put away as much as they possibly can afford to while they're working. Contributions are made on a pre-tax basis, so you are not currently taxed on that amount, and clearly, based on research studies, most people need to save much more than they currently are for retirement. However, what you don't get in the typical 401(k) plan is an unlimited choice of investment options within the plan; you will be limited to what fund options your employer chose to include.

Now, when you leave that job or retire, if you open an IRA to roll over those plan assets, or roll over to your existing IRA if you have one, you get to decide exactly what you'd like to invest those funds into, such as individual bonds, individual stocks, mutual funds, annuities (such as the principal-protected fixed index annuity discussed earlier) or exchange-traded funds, just to name a few. If the IRA language allows it, you can also invest more intricately, such as in structured products and private placements. Directing your own IRA rollover account opens up an entire world of options for you to invest in. That being said, I obviously highly recommend you consult with a financial advisor before making investment decisions that will impact your life in retirement. This is one decision you don't want to go it alone on, and you shouldn't have to, given the amount of good advisors available to help.

The more choices you have, the better. It's your own personal retirement account. That's what it stands for — *i*ndividual *r*etirement *a*ccount. It's your own personally directed account. You decide what to invest in. There is total clarity on fees, investment types or options. You can essentially do what you want.

I've also seen many instances where an employee leaves one company to join another and simply transfers their 401(k) from their previous employer's plan into their new employer's plan.

What have you done here? You simply took one plan with very limited options and moved it into another limited-option plan.

Again, when you leave a job, take the money with you by rolling over your funds to an IRA. It belongs to you and you can invest the way you want to in order to control your own retirement destiny.

Expenses and Fees

Another reason to take your 401(k) plan assets with you by rollover is the expense ratio many fund companies charge within these plans. I was stunned at how high some of these are. Keep in mind, even a 1.75 percent annual management fee, which I think is very high, does not include any trading fees a mutual fund may incur buying and selling shares during the year. Some of these internal trading fees can be very expensive and costly for employees, since they directly affect the net rate of return they earn. Most 401(k) participants I've spoken with over the years have no idea these fees even exist!

Also, 401(k) plans pay an annual fee to the third-party administrator of the plan and this fee is generally passed on to all participants. It doesn't make any sense to pay your portion of these fees for limited investment options when you're not even an active participant of the plan any longer.

I've noticed a growing trend the past few years of 401(k) plans utilizing group mutual funds rather than the typical individual fund option, where one can look up a daily market quote to track performance. When reviewing a new client's 401(k) plan assets, I often use Morningstar X-Ray to review such items as performance, expenses, fund style, management team and underlying investments of the particular fund(s) they're invested in. The problem with group funds is they tend not to have a standard or comparable trading symbol, making it difficult to obtain this information. If you own an individual stock or mutual fund it's easy to obtain a daily price on that security, as well as performance history.

Another primary advantage of IRA rollovers is the simplicity of management. By the time you retire, you have all of your retirement assets together, and not in 401(k)s from three, four or more companies spread all over the place.

By moving your money to your IRA, you are controlling fees and increasing your investment options, while also achieving asset consolidation, simplicity and personal control.

Another important investment tool, called the "in-service 401(k) rollover," allows current employees to roll over a portion of their plan assets to their own personalized IRA, allowing far greater investment options and better control of annual fees/charges. The majority of 401(k) plans currently allow some form of in-service rollovers for their employee participants. Your financial advisor should review your plan thoroughly. You should also check with your human resources department or 401(k) plan administrator to find out if your plan allows for in-service rollovers.

Required Minimum Distributions

While the U.S. government certainly encourages its citizens to save for their own retirement through the use of pre-tax accounts, such as traditional IRAs, 401(k)s, 403(b)s and other types of pension plans, keep in mind they also have that pesky tax code provision called required minimum distributions (RMDs). After reaching the age of 70 ½, the IRS will require individuals to withdraw a minimum amount of their qualified retirement account funds every year, and pay taxes on those withdrawals. The required withdrawal amount is determined by a person's age and account balance at the end of each year.

The Internal Revenue Service is clear that you have to include the value of all your qualified retirement assets at year end. They don't care which account you take the money from, but the more traditional IRAs, 401(k)s and other pension accounts you have, the more complicated it may become. Many people in the past used to do a lot of CD-rate shopping for their annual IRA contributions, and as a result may have ended up with accounts all over the place — 15 or 20 accounts at various banks, plus various 401(k)s and possibly a profit-sharing plan as well. This may create a logistics nightmare calculating accurate year-end total balances as sometimes accounts get forgotten and left out of the equation. The IRS may impose up to a whopping 50 percent penalty on all RMD shortages not distributed during any required year! Account consolidation greatly reduces the risk of this ever happening to you.

Flexibility

One of the biggest drawbacks to the 401(k) is the lack of flexibility when it comes to retirement withdrawals. The vast majority provide limited options on how to receive your pension income when that time arrives, and very few plans that I've ever reviewed provide cost-of-living adjustments built in. We all know inflation exists, and the costs of goods and services will rise each year, therefore it becomes critical that any sound retirement income plan account for the need of increasing monthly income, especially with people living as long as they are now.

If you are among the majority of Americans worried about future inflation and outliving your income, your retirement income plan must be mainly comprised of investments providing guaranteed income for as long as you live, adjusted for inflation! Most 401(k) plans simply don't offer that guaranteed protection.

That's why I generally recommend that my clients invest a portion of their retirement assets into an annuity if they don't have a traditional pension plan. Guaranteed income for life, with cost-of-living increases built in, is a key part of any person's successful retirement income plan, and the only way to achieve that outside of a traditional company pension is with an annuity.

CHAPTER TEN

Creating an Income Plan

People spend 20, 30 or even 40 years saving for retirement. The successful ones put a lot of time and energy into that. But, whether you've saved a half-million, $1 million or $5 million, unless you have created a realistic income plan or road map, it could potentially be all for naught.

Am I being too negative? Not in the least bit. If you fail to work with a qualified financial advisor to figure out how to turn that nest egg into a lifetime stream of retirement income, you risk what many people say in surveys is their biggest fear. And that, my friends, is the fear of outliving their retirement savings.

I like to start with the basics with my clients. So, what exactly is a retirement income plan and how do you get one?

In the very basic sense, a retirement income plan is a written plan that shows you how you will turn that retirement nest egg that you worked so hard to save into the income you will need once you are no longer drawing a paycheck.

What are the dangers if you don't have a written income plan? The biggest ones are that you overspend and run out of money, or that your required monthly expenses will be greater than the income you can safely generate from your investments, so you'll have to dip into your principal each month to cover them. Either scenario makes it highly likely that you will deplete your retirement funds should you live longer than you anticipated — quite a scary thought since we obviously would rather not have to bet against our own longevity.

So, how much retirement income will you need every month to live comfortably? Well, that's going to depend on your individual circumstances, desires, activities and monthly budget your financial advisor helps you create. Please refer to the importance of creating a budget in retirement section in an earlier chapter.

You probably see or hear various television and radio commercials touting your "magic number" for retiring comfortably. Some say it will take a cool million dollars. Others quote a percentage of your current income.

The truth of the matter is, it's not about a certain lump sum of accumulated assets that will provide the retirement of your dreams. Rather, it's about the amount of "inflation-protected income" you will need to generate beginning on day one of retirement. Only after knowing your required monthly income amount can it be accurately determined what amount of funds you will actually need in order to be able to provide that income.

No one takes all the money they've saved for retirement and sticks it under their mattress to be pulled out in bits and pieces as needed. Obviously that strategy would never provide peace-of-mind that you wouldn't outlive your money.

Retirement shouldn't be a crapshoot; it must be planned for properly and sufficiently ahead of time, taking all possible known variables into account. What if you live to the ripe old age of 95? Or your spouse becomes one of a growing population of seniors over the age of 100?

Your retirement income plan absolutely must provide two basic elements. The first is guaranteed income for as long as you and your spouse may live, and the second is inflation protection to avoid erosion of buying power. In my experience, there is no such thing as a successful, properly planned retirement income plan without those two factors built in! Inflation can be the silent killer to any successful, enjoyable retirement. We know from history that items we buy today will cost far more in the future. This holds true as well for those pesky monthly utility bills, property taxes, health care and insurance needs, and so forth.

The income plan becomes a major section of your overall financial plan. When my firm prepares an individualized plan for one of our clients, we employ a variety of computerized software programs that will project various scenarios. Using these programs allows us the necessary ability to project optimal ways for our clients to take their Social Security benefits, as well as their retirement income, based on the various accounts they have. People are generally not aware that they should withdraw from certain asset classes before others. We review all of their current assets and develop a plan to show which accounts they should withdraw from first, and why it matters.

For example, in many cases a Roth IRA and any non-qualified investments — which qualify for capital gains tax treatment — are usually the best options to start taking income from first. That's because withdrawals taken after age 59 ½ from a Roth IRA are tax-free (remember, you already paid taxes on the income before you put it in the Roth), and capital gains tax rates are generally much lower than ordinary income tax rates. To qualify for capital gains tax treatment, you must have held the investment for at least a year and one day.

I recently completed a retirement income plan for a couple. I was able to show them that because they will have adequate income in the first years of retirement, they will be able to comfortably wait until age 70 to start drawing on their Social Security benefits. This is hugely important, since their benefit amount will increase by 8 percent annually, just by deferring from normal retirement age (NRA) to age 70. There is no benefit in waiting beyond age 70 to start taking your Social Security benefits, since no deferral increase is added past that age.

You Must Know What You Can Safely Withdraw

One thing that often surprises me is that people don't seem to understand their accumulated assets need to be turned into regular, reliable income when they retire. They may have built up a sizeable portfolio of stocks, bonds or mutual funds during their "accumulation phase," but now they need that monthly check to replace the paycheck they're no longer earning as a retiree. Quite often, people think they can simply draw 6, 7 or even 8 percent a year from their portfolio, even if it means some of that income may be coming from their investment principal. Realistically, they can't!

Once you go down that path of withdrawing a higher percent than what your investments are actually earning, you're now reducing your principal, which will in turn reduce your future investment earnings even further. If most of your assets during retirement are still exposed to potential market losses, the problem becomes compounded further, since you will be selling shares during a bad market at a lower price to provide your needed income. My experience has taught me that this is a recipe for disaster!

I believe this to be the primary reason many financial advisors like myself are now recommending fixed index annuities be an integral part of any retirement income plan. Because they provide reliable guaranteed income for life, growth potential through index options for inflation protection, all while protecting principal against market loss. The universe of fixed index and hybrid fixed index annuities can be quite complicated, not all of these investment vehicles are created equally. It's very important to work with an advisor who is not only versed with these, but also has access to the very best fixed index annuities offered, since there can be quite a big difference between them.

More than two decades ago, a California financial planner named Bill Bengen founded the "Four Percent Rule" theory, which has been used ever since by most financial advisors as the widely accepted retirement income guideline. This rule of thumb suggests that withdrawing 4 percent of your nest egg the first year of retirement, and increasing that dollar amount each year by inflation to preserve your purchasing power, you will have an 80 to 90 percent assurance that your savings will last at least 30 years. Withdrawing larger percentages than that means you stand a very good chance of running out of money. Obviously any theory or rule of thumb accuracy will depend on exactly which investments people own, as well as the future performance of those investments.

People may also have different needs at different stages of retirement. For example, some retirees may want to plan on taking higher withdrawals earlier in their retirement, and then reduce the amount later.

Think of it this way. When people retire at age 60 or 65, many are generally in good health. They may want to travel, golf, take advantage of hobbies or even visit (spoil) the children and grandchildren while they are physically able to.

When they get to be 75 or 80, they may be inclined to draw less income if they're unable to do as much in the way of activities, or travel.

I recently met with some long-time clients for lunch. In fact, they were among my first clients almost 35 years ago. They were visiting their son in Tampa, and, as always, we get together when they're in town. Due to their age and physical ailments, neither of them can play golf much anymore the way they used to, so they don't need to pay for that country club membership any longer. As you get older, you're more likely to run into more physical and health issues.

That doesn't necessarily mean that everyone will spend less money as they age in retirement. Remember, inflation doesn't go away, and even if you're unable to travel to exotic places or spend money on activities you previously enjoyed, it's very likely you may need to earmark even more funds toward medical or long-term care needs.

People Who Have Not Saved Enough

According to a survey done by the Employee Benefit Research Institute (EBRI) and Greenwald & Associates, more than a third of Americans have less than $1,000 in savings. (That excludes homes and pensions). Sixty percent of Americans have saved less than $25,000.

Less than half — 44 percent — have tried to calculate how much money they'll need to have by the time they retire so they can live a comfortable retirement.

Those numbers agree with my observations over the years. I find that most people have not saved enough money. As a result, they do not have the assets to cover everything they want to do in retirement, including having adequate retirement income.

A lot of people don't realize the amount of years they may have to plan for. Take for example a married couple, both aged 65. There is a 50 percent chance that one of them will still be alive at age 95. That's a lot of retirement-income years to potentially require covering.

Keep in mind that I don't typically sit down with people who have just handed in their retirement papers. Generally, people who come to me are at least a few years away from retirement, so we have at least a little time to fix some things that may need to be addressed.

While it is far better to have planned your retirement many years ahead of time, there are still options available that would help improve the retirement outlook for those people who haven't saved enough:

Reduce Debt

Debt can be a huge problem in retirement. The biggest culprit can be those high-interest credit cards. Mortgage debt and car loans can also be an issue if you don't have enough income to pay them on a monthly basis. (This is not to say that I advise everyone to pay off their mortgage before they retire. That is a case-by-case decision.)

And increasingly, people close to retirement or in retirement also have to deal with college tuition debt because they took out loans or co-signed for their children or grandchildren's education, or perhaps for their own re-education later in life.

What I do tell my clients is they should go into retirement with as little debt as possible. Remember, you won't be getting a paycheck any longer and the money you begin to withdraw from investment accounts needs to go toward paying your expenses in retirement — not to retire old debt.

Reallocate Assets

Sometimes the answer to providing a pre-retiree or retiree the amount of income they need during retirement may be as simple as reallocating their existing assets. Again, depending on the client(s), we may recommend moving them into assets that are safer if they have a more-than-sufficient nest egg. Or, it may require them to take on a little added risk for the potential of earning a higher return if their assets are insufficient to provide their desired income level, and if they still insist on retiring rather than working a little longer. We may also suggest reallocating any growth-oriented investments into more income-producing assets.

Save More While You Still Can

You may be surprised at how many people don't maximize their contributions to their retirement savings plans. This may be one of the best options to make up for lost time and get you where you want to be.

Max out your 401(k) or IRA. Make sure you at least match what your employer is putting into your plan. I see so many people, for example, who have employers that will match their contributions up to 6 percent of their salary, dollar for dollar, and yet they may be only contributing 2 or 3 percent. To me, that's insane, since you're not only turning down free money from your employer, but also paying taxes on those contributions you should have been making to your own retirement account!

You're running out of time, but you still have some opportunities. Take advantage of the age-50-and-over catch-up provisions in your 401(k), 403(b) or IRA accounts. Remember that even if you invest in safer instruments during your retirement, you still need to plan to make your money last for at least 30 years. So, any money you can contribute now will help you in the long term.

Work Longer

Nearly a quarter of American workers said they will have to work beyond age 70, according to a 2016 survey by Willis Towers Watson. Also, a third of those surveyed expect they will retire later than they had previously planned to.

This may not always be an exciting or even a viable option, depending upon your health, but it certainly may be a great way to help your future retirement. You'll not only have a longer time frame for saving more money, but you are also delaying withdrawing money from your nest egg. You're getting twice the bang for your buck!

A lot of people plan to work into those retirement years but are thwarted either by poor health or unexpected forced retirement. So, while staying longer in your current job is generally a good option, people should also look at part-time work or consulting. You may even have a hobby that you can turn into income.

There are organizations like Encore.org and the AARP that help people move into that encore, or second, career when they're done with their first one.

Lower Expectations

This, my friends, is the last resort. If you haven't saved enough money and the other choices discussed aren't possible, you may have to ratchet back your retirement expectations. You may not be able to live in the lifestyle you desire or have been accustomed to. And it's not as simple as just cutting out cable TV.

There are many ways to accomplish this without too drastic of a change in your standard of living, however. You can downsize, or move to a smaller home and use the savings as income. If you live in a high-cost metropolitan area, you may want to move to a smaller town or city with a lower cost of living.

You may have to plan to take only one vacation a year instead of two, or vacation at the local beach, or Florida instead of Hawaii.

There are many ways you can lower your expenses if you lower your expectations.

The point is, even if you haven't saved enough for your retirement, there is no reason to give up hope. There are ways to adapt your retirement to your current assets. It may not be all you've dreamed about, but you can still create a happy, comfortable retirement.

But, whether you think you have saved enough money or not, you need to make sure your financial house is in order while you still have time on your side, so sit down with a financial advisor. The sooner, the better. So, do it now.

CHAPTER ELEVEN

The Importance of Wills, Trusts and Estate Planning

It's hard to fathom that most Americans spend their whole lives trying to accumulate wealth for many reasons, including retirement, yet they fail to plan for what is inevitable: Our demise.

Even more shocking is the list of wealthy and famous individuals who died without even having a simple will prepared during their lifetime. The most recent example that comes to mind is music icon Prince, who died in 2016 at the age of 57.

As of the writing of this book, his estimated fortune stood at over $300 million, yet he failed to have even a simple will drawn up by an attorney to stipulate his wishes as to how his assets should be divided, and amongst whom.

Among other famous individuals who died without having a will, also known as "dying intestate," was our 16th president, Abraham Lincoln, who amazingly we all know was a lawyer before being elected president of the United States. You would think this lack of simple common-sense planning would be rare for celebrities and other wealthy people, since they usually have access to top advisors, planners and attorneys. But take a look at this abbreviated list of people who died with no will in place:

- Iconic rock musicians Jimi Hendrix and Prince
- Reggae legend Bob Marley
- Artist Pablo Picasso
- Entertainer-turned-politician Sony Bono
- Civil rights leader Martin Luther King Jr.
- 3-time All-Pro NFL quarterback Steve McNair

Now, I fully understand that most people just don't want to think about or deal with the subject of death, but let me remind my readers that none of us will ever escape it. I'm sure you've heard the old saying that only two things in life are guaranteed: death and taxes. Well, it's true!

Still, more than half (55 percent) of American adults do not have a will or other estate plan in place, according to LexisNexis.

Those numbers have remained relatively steady for the last 20 years, even as the number of other estate planning documents (such as medical directives) has increased.

The numbers are even higher among minorities: 68 percent of African American adults and 74 percent of Hispanic adults do not have a will, according to the survey.

A will is a simple, painless process of having an attorney draw up a legal document that lets you decide who should receive which of your assets after your death. It's fairly inexpensive, especially when compared to probate court costs, should you die without one. It also allows you to name guardians who will take care of your dependent children. Do you really want a probate court judge deciding not only who gets what assets of yours, but who will watch over your children as well?

There are certain asset classifications that allow you to name beneficiaries that take precedence over a will, such as IRA accounts, pension plans, life insurance policies and annuities, to name a few.

You should periodically review your current beneficiary designations to make sure they reflect your current wishes, particularly after any life-changing events, such as divorce, the death of an existing beneficiary or the birth of another child.

With a will, you also name your executor, which is the person who will be in charge of settling your estate after your death. Make sure you name an individual who understands the tasks involved, including distributing your property, filing tax returns and dealing with any potential creditors.

The person you decide to name as your executor should be someone you completely trust, but also must be willing to accept this huge responsibility.

What Is Estate Planning?

To put it simply, estate planning involves deciding how you want your assets distributed after you die or become unable to make your own financial decisions. This can range from a simple written plan to a much more complicated plan, so it's best to consult a financial advisor as well as an estate planning attorney.

Regardless of your net worth, it's important that you have at least a basic estate plan in place. You get to name your beneficiaries and make your wishes legally binding. Some estate planning involves minimizing future taxes that may be imposed on one's estate upon death, while other plans provide peace of mind, knowing your financial house is in order. An estate plan may include a will, a living will, keeping beneficiary forms up to date, a health care proxy or some type of trust.

Dying Without a Will

Dying without a will (intestate) means you have no say over who receives your assets, and you can leave your heirs and the courts the complex and costly job of wrangling over who should get which of your assets.

Then your assets go into probate, which can be an expensive and extended legal process that determines who inherits your estate. It can take anywhere from a few months to years, depending on how complicated the estate is.

Intestacy laws vary considerably from state to state. But, in general, if you die and leave a spouse and kids, your assets will be split between your surviving spouse and the children. For single people, the state is likely to decide who among your blood relatives will inherit your estate.

Probate

Probate is the legal process that occurs after a person dies. The probate court system must first validate that the will is authentic, and then proceed to distribute the estate among the heirs. When there is not a valid will, the probate court must decide, depending on the laws of the state, how the assets are distributed.

The website *LegalZoom* cites the Wisconsin State Bar as saying a "complicated will" could take more than two years to probate. But even a simple one may take at least six months.

The amount of time is similar in other states, according to the American Bar Association. Why does probate take so long? Because most states have minimum periods of time that creditors are allowed to respond. During that time, the probated estate cannot be distributed.

A Living Will

This legal document establishes your choices for the kind of life-sustaining medical intervention you wish, or do not want, in the event that you become terminally ill or are unable to communicate. It is often combined with a health care proxy, meanwhile, which authorizes someone to make medical decisions on your behalf.

The lack of proper paperwork and authentication can be a major headache for the many adult children who are providing care for an aging parent. Princeton Survey Research Associates International conducted telephone interviews with 1,000 adults living in the U.S. in 2015 and found the majority of adult children are not adequately informed of the documents required to ensure they can care for and assist their aging parents medically or financially if they become ill or incapacitated.

More than half, or 54.2 percent, said they had no idea where their parents kept their wills and living trust documents. A whopping 58 percent said they had no idea what the documents said or did.

What Is a Trust?

A trust is a legal entity that lets you put conditions on how certain assets are distributed upon your death. They can also help minimize gift and estate taxes.

Revocable trust: This allows you to retain control of all the assets in the trust, and as a result you are free to revoke or change the terms of the trust at any time.

Irrevocable trust: The assets you place in this trust no longer belong to you. Typically, you cannot make changes without the beneficiaries' consents. However, the appreciated assets are not subject to estate taxes.

As you can see, there are many different options involved with estate planning, whether simple or complex, but it's extremely important to make these decisions while you still can. We all must come to grips with our own mortality and proper planning will make things much easier for our loved ones when that inevitable time arrives.

CHAPTER TWELVE

In Conclusion

It is my sincere hope that, after reading this book and sharing my 35 years of experience in the financial services industry, you will be on the right path to achieving the retirement you dream about.

I can't stress enough, with the complexities of today's investment markets along with the myriad of investment vehicles available for your retirement nest egg, how pivotal it is to work with the right professional financial advisor who can help make the entire planning process easier for you and far more accurate in the long run.

It will take a serious commitment of time and effort on your part as well as your advisor's, especially in the beginning planning stages. But your retirement success depends largely on the amount and quality of effort invested when establishing your financial plan. The earlier you begin this planning process, the more time you'll have to make any necessary changes in your spending or savings habits that can put you on the right path.

In this book, we have discussed many of the important retirement planning areas you should be focusing on, including:

- Putting away enough money in your earlier years into the proper account types

- Preparing a quality budget that can help you get a handle on your expenses
- Reducing debt prior to retirement
- Determining realistic retirement goals
- Maximizing future Social Security benefits using ideal timing methods
- Having a quality plan in place for a lifetime of retirement income
- Including cost-of-living adjustments (COLAs) to avoid erosion of future buying power
- Having proper legal documents in place to avoid putting your heirs through unnecessary turmoil after your death

One of the greatest passions in my life is helping good people achieve the quality of retirement they've dreamed about for years, while getting to see the looks of contentment on their faces and knowing that I played an integral part in their retirement bliss. When you've worked with people for over 30 years, you can't help but become friends with them along with being their financial advisor. I've built up some amazing relationships and personal friendships with the vast majority of my clients, including their children and grandchildren now.

I have incorporated a simple, basic philosophy with my business all these years, and that is to always put the clients' needs first! Acting in my clients' best interests — also known as acting in a fiduciary capacity — simply means that any and all recommendations I make to them are to be for their best interest and not mine. Like with any successful, long-standing business model, the customers must always come first. Those not willing to think about building long-term customer relationships by preferring to focus on their own short-term needs will not stand the test of time, and may subject themselves to the wrath of financial industry regulators, as well.

Let's review in a little more detail what we have covered in this book. You should feel comfortable going back for reference or reminders.

Chapter 1

Becoming the Best at What I Do.

Hopefully, you really got to know me in the first chapter. I discussed my family and what motivated me to get into financial planning in the first place. That's important, because my roots in Upstate New York and my beginning experiences with clients have had a dramatic and sustained impact on the way I do business today.

Chapter highlights: The only real financial planning my father ever ascribed to was dreaming of the day he would retire, perhaps at 65. Ironically, the factory where he had worked was closed before he would have turned 62. He owned no personal life insurance and only minimal group insurance through Bethlehem Steel. He had no personal savings, nor any retirement savings other than what his employer contributed to. That, as my mother found out the hard way, was not nearly enough to survive on.

More than anything, that experience shaped what kind of financial planner I would be. I am determined to see that my customers are more prepared than my family was.

Chapter 2

Finding the "Perfect" Financial Planner

Chapter highlights: In this chapter we dealt with what it takes to find the perfect financial advisor. Disco diva Grace Jones had a song in 1986: *"I'm Not Perfect (But I'm Perfect for You)."* That's what you are looking for in a financial advisor: One that is perfect for *you* and one who meets your individual needs.

And remember my six rules:
1. Do I like you?
2. Do I trust you?
3. Are you an experienced advisor?
4. What sets you apart from other financial advisors?
5. Do you have my best interests in mind?
6. Are you an independent advisor who can offer me unbiased solutions?

Chapter 3

Investment Options Made Simple

Here we dealt with the importance of diversification (and the dangers of not having a diversified portfolio) and I explained various investment options.

Chapter highlights: In layman's terms, don't put all your eggs in one basket. I can't think of a better example of how devastating this can be than the Enron bankruptcy of 2001. Many employees of this energy company behemoth were being told by management how great the company was doing. As a result, many invested most or all of their 401(k) retirement money in company stock rather than other options offered by the plan.

What resulted from this debacle? For Enron employees who chose to invest most or all of their 401(k) retirement money in their company's stock, it was a total loss. There were reports at that time of employees getting ready to retire from Enron thinking they had well over $1 million in their 401(k) plans, only to find they were completely wiped out. If that wasn't bad enough news, many not only couldn't retire as previously planned, but now had to find new jobs as well, adding insult to injury.

Chapter 4

Roadblocks to a Successful Retirement

We discussed how we have gone from a world dominated by company pension plans to a new world order dominated by direct-contribution plans, or 401(k)s. With that comes a tremendous responsibility — and it is your responsibility.

Chapter highlights: The burden has now shifted from the employer to you, the employee. Today, about 18 percent of full-time workers have pensions, down from 35 percent in the early 1990s, according to the Bureau of Labor Statistics.

Managing your retirement portfolio is certainly not easy and there are so many things that can go wrong. That's one reason it is so important to find a great financial advisor to help you.

Chapter 5

Using the Tax Code to Your Advantage

Here we focused on tax-advantaged accounts such as 401(k)s, 403(b)s, IRAs and other retirement accounts. It is important to know the differences and which ones may work best for you.

Chapter highlights: A big part of any person's tax strategy should be tax-advantaged savings plans. They range from IRAs to 401(k)s and 403(b)s. What you need to know is there is a tax benefit associated with saving in these accounts. I explained the various types of retirement accounts, the tax benefits of each and some of their characteristics and intricacies.

Chapter 6

Protecting What You Have: Risk vs. Reward

There is no doubt about it: There are risks in the stock market. But that doesn't mean you should not participate. It means you need to understand the risks vs. the rewards — and when you need to reduce those risks as you plan for retirement.

Chapter highlights: Stocks have up years and down years. And while a portfolio filled with stocks is the best investment you can make over the long term, as you get closer to retirement you must ramp down on stocks to reduce your risk.

The thinking is pretty basic here. A 40-year-old has maybe 20 years to make up for those "bad" years in the market. But a 55-year-old who plans to retire at 62 has only a few years. It gets worse if he or she is forced into an earlier retirement than anticipated.

Chapter 7

Understanding Annuities 101

Annuities are so misunderstood these days; we dealt with why they may be such a necessary part of your portfolio.

Chapter highlights: Today, annuities can factor into almost every retirement plan because they are virtually the only investment available on the planet that guarantees a lifetime income for you, and possibly your spouse, regardless of how long you live. That eliminates longevity risk, which we talked about earlier in this chapter. People worry they will run out of money while they are still alive and either have to go back to work or live below their desired standard of living. A successful retirement plan has to include income that is guaranteed every month.

Chapter 8

Social Security

There are still some financial planners who make the mistake of not including Social Security as part of your financial plan. It is an integral part of your retirement and you must know how it fits within your portfolio.

Chapter highlights: As you now know, there are many difficult decisions to be made when you are approaching retirement. Hopefully, you have already made some of the most difficult — picking a financial advisor, knowing whether to stay put or buy a new retirement home, and deciding when you want retire.

But Social Security may be one of the hardest — and most complicated.

That's why it's so important to study and prepare — and not wait until you are facing a deadline to make your decision. Study your options when you are still in your 50s, and utilize some professional knowledge.

Chapter 9

Rollovers

This chapter, you remember, dealt with what to do when you leave a job. We are a mobile nation, and thus we generally have five or six jobs by the time we retire. It's important to not lose track of your 401(k) plans.

Chapter highlights: I'd like to answer a question I get from clients and potential clients all the time: When I leave my job (or retire), should I leave my 401(k), transfer it to my new company's plan, or withdraw the money and open an IRA?

My answer is an unequivocal: Do not leave it with a company you have otherwise cut ties with. Take your money when you leave. One advisor suggested you complete the paperwork on your last day of work, at the earliest, and begin to move it to an IRA. That way you insure that it's done.

It is, after all, *your* money.

Chapter 10

Creating an Income Plan

This is the part that many people find the most difficult. You have to change from the saving mode to the income mode. And you'd better have a financial advisor who knows what he or she is doing to help you with that.

Chapter highlights: People spend 20, 30 or even 40 years saving for retirement. The successful ones put a lot of time and energy into that. But, whether you've saved a half-million, $1 million or $5 million, unless you have created a realistic income plan or roadmap, it could potentially be all for naught.

Chapter 11

The Importance of Wills, Trusts and Estate Planning

We put it off as long as we can. But it is really important to not leave your heirs without a plan for what to do when you die. You can dramatically decrease the stress on your loved ones if you take care of estate planning and living wills in advance. I know it's not a pleasant thought, but it is completely necessary.

Chapter highlights: A will is the simple, painless process of having an attorney draw up a legal document that lets you decide who should receive which of your assets after your death. It's fairly inexpensive, especially when compared to probate court costs should you die without one. It also allows you to name guardians who will take care of your dependent children. Do you really want a probate court judge deciding not only who gets what assets of yours but who will watch over your children, as well?

With that, I would like to leave you with three pieces of advice.

1. Remember Bernie Madoff!

As with most business industries, the financial services field has been shown to have had its share of slick talking charlatans. Most Americans are familiar with the Bernie Madoff case, as it received a huge amount of media coverage. Madoff pleaded guilty in March 2009 of running a multi-billion dollar Ponzi scheme and received a prison sentence of 150 years along with over $17 billion dollars in fines. He was a former non-executive chairman of the NASDAQ stock market who, while running his own private equity firm, admitted to scheming investors — including family and friends — out of billions of dollars of their hard-earned assets, mostly to benefit his lavish lifestyle. I bring this well-known case example up, not to scare you, but rather to advise diligence on your part as to which financial advisor you choose to work with.

2. Do your homework and check references before you hire a financial advisor.

Do some homework before you choose the advisor you're going to be working with. You can find much information online nowadays, or ask friends and co-workers whom they work with and if they're satisfied with that advisor's recommendations and level of service. Make sure you interview potential candidates to see who would be the best fit for you, which independent advisor will be able to provide the types of products and services you require, along with unbiased recommendations, and whom you feel you would be able to build a long-lasting trust and relationship with.

3. I am here to help you.
We would be honored to serve you.

I've been fortunate enough to have had many articles I've written published by some of our industry's leading financial outlets, including NY Daily News, Investor's Business Daily and American Express, to name a few. I also hold the designation of Certified Retirement Counselor (CRC) from the International Foundation for Retirement Education, also known as InFRE, which places high degrees of requirements in the areas of experience and examination, ethics and continuing education. Working with the largest — and, in my opinion, the best — independent financial marketing organization in the country, along with being a Series 24 registered securities principal, has allowed me the unique ability to offer unbiased recommendations to all of my clients as to the best investment and/or insurance solutions to fit their individual needs. We would be honored to provide these same services and financial solutions to you and your family should you so desire. Feel free to reach out to me, I'd be happy to answer any questions you may have or discuss your individual plan — thank you for reading my book, I hope it helped you!

Brett King, CRC

Elite Financial Associates
550 N. Reo Street, Suite 300
Tampa, Florida 33609

800-889-3017
brett@elitefinancialassociates.com
www.EliteFinancialAssociates.com

www.ingramcontent.com/pod-product-compliance
Lightning Source LLC
Chambersburg PA
CBHW070258190526
45169CB00001B/457